Adaptation Online

STUDIES IN NEW MEDIA

Series Editor: John Allen Hendricks,
Stephen F. Austin State University

This series aims to advance the theoretical and practical understanding of the emergence, adoption, and influence of new technologies. It provides a venue to explore how New Media technologies are changing the media landscape in the twenty-first century.

TITLES IN SERIES:

The Twenty-First-Century Media Industry: Economic and Managerial Implications in the Age of New Media, edited by John Allen Hendricks
Blogging: How Our Private Thoughts Went Public, by Kristin Roeschenthaler Wolfe
Beyond New Media: Discourse and Critique in a Polymediated Age, edited by Art Herbig, Andrew F. Herrmann, and Adam W. Tyma
Communicating User Experience: Applying Local Strategies Research to Digital Media Design, edited by Trudy Milburn
Navigating New Media Networks: Understanding and Managing Communication Challenges in a Networked Society, by Bree McEwan
Globalization's Impact on Cultural Identity Formation: Queer Diasporic Males in Cyberspace, by Ahmet Atay
Social Media: Culture and Identity, edited by Kehbuma Langmia and Tia Tyree
Swipe Right for Love: The Impact of Social Media in Modern Romantic Relationships, edited by Narissra M. Punyanunt-Carter and Jason S. Wrench
The Evolution and Social Impact of Video Game Economics, edited by Casey B. Hart
New Media and Digital Pedagogy: Enhancing the Twenty-First-Century Classroom, edited by Michael G. Strawser
Adaptation Online: Creating Memes, Sweding Movies, and Other Digital Performances, by Lyndsay Michalik Gratch

Contents

Acknowledgments

This book grew from the research I began with my doctoral dissertation, "'Post Your Version Here!: Performances in/of Online, Non-Commercial, Video-to-Video Adaptations," published by Louisiana State University and Agricultural and Mechanical College (2014). I owe special thanks to Trish Suchy, along with Michael Bowman, Rachel Hall, and Kate Jensen for their guidance as I began this research. An earlier multimedia version of chapter 2 was also published as "How Antoine Dodson and the Bed Intruder Keep Climbin' in Our Windows: Viral Video Appropriation as Performance," in *Liminalities: A Journal of Performance Studies* 10.3/4 (2014). I would like to thank Michael LeVan for his help throughout that process.

Each chapter has been revised and updated for this book. I thank John Allen Hendricks, Nicolette Amstutz, and James Hamill for their advice and help in readying the manuscript for publication. I thank Craig Gingrich-Philbrook for his thoughtful, thorough, and precise suggestions as I completed this project. I thank Johanna Broussard, Lisa Flanagan, Anna Marsden, K. McClure, Roy Michalik Jr., and Jennifer Tuder for their efficient and timely proof-reading of chapter drafts. I must also thank Mark Michalik for introducing me to my first-ever internet meme (the "Star Wars Kid"), and its many adaptations.

Thank you to my fellow sweders, including the late John LeBret, Lauren Leist, and Mike Rold for their amazing performances in *Dirty Harry—SWEDED*. Special thanks, as well, to all who have reviewed earlier versions of chapter 5, and who have participated in the Sweding panels I organized for the National Communication Association's 2015 and 2016 conferences: Jason Munsell, Mindy Fenske, Trish Suchy, Tracy Stephenson Shaffer, Anna Marsden, Stephanie Kilgore Heath, Lisa Flanagan, Melanie O'Meara, Nichole Nicholson, Samuel Sloan, David Terry, Amber Johnson, Dre Betancourt, Lindsay Greer, Emily Graves, Michael LeVan, Austin McDonald, Nicole Costantini, Colin Whitworth, Andrea Vickery, Zach Vickery, Sarah Jackson Shipman, Sarah Friday, Bryan McCann, and Josh Gunn.

Ariel Gratch, thank you for everything. From playing the title role in *Dirty Harry—SWEDED* (and the leading role[s] in all the other Sweded movies we have made), to your endless reading of chapter drafts and incredibly helpful suggestions. Thank you for your love, support, honesty, and perfect sense of humor.

Chapter 5 is dedicated to John.
This book is for Raphael.

ONE

Online Video-to-Video Adaptation

Since the early days of internet video technology and person-to-person file sharing, my younger brother Mark and I have communicated largely through videos. Not videos we created; videos made by other people. Funny videos. Silly videos. Shocking videos. Ridiculous videos. Creative videos. Over a decade ago, we communicated through videos by sending each other links to websites via email. More often, though, we would communicate this way in person, spending hours sitting together at a computer, sharing the latest, funniest, internet videos—one-upping each other with, "Well, have you seen . . . ?!" hoping to make the other person laugh. This was one way that we communicated our shared interests, our shared sense of humor, and our mutual desire to laugh and have fun. But we weren't just interested in the funny videos. We also spent quite a bit of time watching "versions" of funny internet videos, when these existed. Adaptations, per se. Variations on a theme. In 2003, for example, my brother introduced me to the (now [in]famous) "Star Wars Kid" video and its many adaptations. We watched several hours of the Star Wars Kid, in one to five minute spurts, all in one sitting. When a new version of the Star Wars Kid video was posted somewhere online, it was a point of pride between the two of us to be the first one to discover and share it.

"Star Wars Kid" was the nickname given to Ghyslain Raza, the Canadian teenager "who filmed himself fighting against imaginary sentries with a golf-ball retriever, as though it were a double-sided light saber wielded by the antagonist Darth Maul in *Star Wars: Episode I*."[1] In November 2002, Raza recorded this short movie of himself "pretend fighting with a club in his high school studio," but then "forgot to take the [video] home with him."[2] In April 2003, three of Raza's classmates discovered the video at school and uploaded it to the file-sharing network Kazaa. Soon after, other internet users began uploading new versions of Raza's video, with added light saber and sound effects, to additional file-sharing networks. These adaptations of Raza's video included, among others, a version where Raza is seen fighting his own clone, a version where Raza is labeled a "drunken Jedi," a version that places Raza in a canoe, and a *Matrix* version that uses slow motion video effects. These videos were all initially circulated several years before YouTube even existed, and thus "the Star Wars Kid phenomenon may be seen as one of the first instances of a massively consumed online video, a forebear to a now robust online video culture supporting a much deeper dimension for regular feedback . . . and parody."[3] This video was not just *consumed*, though. The Star Wars Kid video was a generative phenomenon that inspired a legion of video adaptations.

My brother and I still communicate through video sharing, and these days we have a *much* wider range of videos to choose from. Feedback and parody, meanwhile, are just the tip of the iceberg, in terms of how online video adaptation has progressed over the last decade. From creatively but "incorrectly" subtitling movies, to remaking and sharing five-minute-no-budget versions of movies, to performing parodies of viral videos, to creating musical remixes of local news footage, internet users have demonstrated how creative adaptation using video and internet technology has become a form of communication, an everyday art, a skill set, and a means of sociopolitical involvement. These creators and adaptors physically perform in their own videos, and they make videos that work performatively online. Negotiating the slippery spaces between copyright, creativity, and cultural commentary, they adapt nontraditional texts in myriad ways, and find spaces to share these adaptations online, despite (for most) a lack of financial return for their creative work.

In this book, I analyze several significant online video-to-video adaptation trends, to show how internet video memes and "sweded" movies are dependent upon performances of adaptation. I focus on four case studies, including adaptations of two local news segments ("Antoine Dodson warns a PERP on LIVE TV!!!" [2010], and "Sweet Brown: No Time for Bronchitis" [2012]), the *Downfall* meme (i.e., "Hitler reacts to" or "Hitler finds out" videos), and the phenomenon of "sweded" cinema. As these case studies represent types of adaptation that do not fit well into contemporary theories of adaptation, I outline a glossary of strategies of online video-to-video adaptation to help a multidisciplinary audience better understand how internet users are "novelizing" traditional notions of the processes and products of adaptation.

Here, I am using the terms "novel" and "novelizing" in the Bakhtinian sense. As Katerina Clark and Michael Holquist explain, "Bakhtin assigns the term 'novel' to whatever form of expression within a given . . . system reveals the limits of that system as inadequate, imposed, or arbitrary. . . . Because the fundamental features of any culture are inscribed in its texts . . . 'novelness' can work to undermine the official high culture of any society."[4] Studying these videos as performance texts allows me to map more thoroughly the mostly uncharted terrain of online video adaptation, elucidate the limits of and expand upon contemporary theories of adaptation, show how these types of adaptation create, sustain, and/or upend contemporary culture, and clarify some of the major problems and paradoxes of current US copyright law as it pertains to online video adaptation.

CONNECTING PARTICIPATORY CULTURE, MEMETICS, AND ADAPTATION

In my mapping, I begin with the relevance of *participatory culture*. In his book *Convergence Culture,* media scholar Henry Jenkins defines participatory culture as a culture "in which fans and other consumers are invited to actively participate in the creation and circulation of new content."[5] Jenkins expands: "The power of participation comes not from destroying commercial culture but from writing over it, modding it [sic], amending it, expanding it, adding greater diversity of perspective, and then recirculating it, feeding it back into the mainstream media."[6] In a participatory media culture, we communicate with each other by using media to create and respond, and in doing so we are also shaping and changing our culture. Rather than encouraging users to simply interact with media (e.g., change the television channel, or click a link online), participatory media gives users agency in the production and distribution of cultural goods. A participatory media culture thus relies on more complex user performances than older, more traditional forms of mass media. Through performances of adaptation, users keep the participatory media cycle moving, while also physically, intellectually, and/or emotionally inserting themselves into said cycle. With every adaptation they make, creators make new meanings from and build upon previous performances of the material with which they are working.

While some online video adaptations might be an attempted means toward an economic end, many more seem to be creative acts with no intended financial goals. Rather, these adaptations are *responses* to popular cultural goods, and are themselves (sometimes popular) cultural goods. Culture, as defined by media scholar John Fiske, is "the constant process of producing meanings of and from our social experience. . . . Such meanings necessarily produce a social identity for the people involved."[7] According to Fiske, popular culture "is made by various formations of subordinated or disempowered people out of the resources, both discursive and material, that are provided by the social system that disempowers them."[8] Further, when viewing media, we activate certain meanings or contradictions in texts above others to "serve [our own] cultural interests." In the act (i.e., performance) of viewing, audiences bring, and are thus influenced by, their "material social existence" and "their cultural experience of other texts."[9]

Popular culture texts also offer space for creativity in adaptation, like "parody, subversion [and] inversion."[10] These types of creative adaptations make statements and create new meanings beyond those that might be inferred from the original text, and can thus be used to communicate their producer's position within and beliefs about existing power structures. Hence, in a participatory media culture, we adapt popular culture texts to both *make* and *make sense out of* culture. Online videos are fertile ground for adaptation, and the technology we use to view and adapt these videos is more affordable and accessible than ever. Meanwhile, YouTube is only one example of many online performance platforms that try to retain the appearance of having a generally open public stance toward video-to-video adaptation—that is, as long as the adaptations in question do not threaten YouTube's business model.

Fiske also posits that derivative texts (again, *adaptations*) exist in relation to other texts and current power structures. Thus, these adaptations resist or proliferate social structures of dominance and subordination. By creating a video adaptation, spectators-turned-producers are navigating and/or negotiating their places within complex social power structures, regardless of their intentions. Text adaptation in general indicates that the producers are aware, at some level, of themselves as socially situated within a larger cultural construct. The producer's method or style of adaptation, in addition to the relative content of the original and "derivative" videos, shows the extent of his or her awareness. Fiske theorizes that while the meaning of a text can be hard to pin down, we might address this by "shift[ing] our focus from the text to its moments of reading."[11] In other words, to determine a video's possible meanings, studying how people are adapting (and by extension *reading*) a video within specific social and historical constructs would prove more fruitful than analyzing the video on its own. Close readings of video-to-video adaptations, along with an analysis of the similarities and differences among these videos, can provide "valuable clues to the readings that a particular culture or subculture is likely to produce."[12] Further, regardless of the efficacy of the individual videos, prevailing motifs and aesthetic commonalities among the adaptations of a single video might indicate what creators specifically value and/or oppose in the video they have chosen to adapt. Finally, trends among the adaptations of a single base text should reveal larger underlying values and power structures that are being propagated or challenged. In other words, analyzing video texts that fans and others have made either from or about a movie (or any type of video text, several of which I consider in this book) can give us a new and different way of understanding said movie or video, the culture that it *comes from,* and also the culture it *produces*. These types of analyses offer insights into film and video cultures that any extended analysis of an "original" work simply cannot, regardless of the analytical methodology employed. Additionally, making *our own* version or adaptation of a movie or video text (an idea which I explore in depth in chapter 5) gives us even further insight into where we situate *ourselves* in relation to popular culture: our unique beliefs, tastes, senses of humor, biases, and even our privileges are exposed when we adapt a video text.

Thus, in this book, I analyze video-to-video adaptations as individual texts in terms of their "vertical intertextuality," or their relations to the original video, and their "horizontal intertextuality," or their potential relations to each other.[13] Of course, my interpretations of what cultural commentary the videos might be making on their own and/or in relation to each other are undoubtedly affected by my own experiences and personal subjectivity. At the same time, taking note of common trends and motifs among the adaptations (particularly specific attempts at reproducing or changing the original visual or spoken text) reveals on a larger scale *how* people are reading/using the original video, regardless of *what* I interpret the adaptations to be implicitly or explicitly saying.

Some of these video adaptations might be more easily referred to as "internet memes." The term meme was coined by evolutionary biologist Richard Dawkins in his book *The Selfish Gene* to explain the spread of ideas and cultural phenomena using evolutionary principles.[14] Examples of cultural memes in *The Selfish Gene* included melodies, catch phrases, and fashion. The term has more recently become an internet buzzword, according to media scholar Jean Burgess, who states:

> In popular usage, the term[s] "Internet meme" [and "viral"] are . . . very loosely applied biological metaphors, appropriated from the various attempts to develop a science of cultural transmission based on evolutionary theory that have been unfolding for decades. The contested field of 'memetics' is the best-known, but by no means only, strand of this kind of thinking, which began with Richard Dawkins's proposal in *The Selfish Gene* of the "meme" as the corresponding cultural unit to the biological gene.[15]

These terms ("meme" and "viral") have been broadly applied to internet phenomena including photos, videos, and songs that are widely appropriated and creatively adapted by internet users. Internet memes are "faddish" jokes or practices "that become widely imitated. . . . Internet 'memes' [also] appear to spread and replicate 'virally'–that is, they appear to spread and mutate via distributed networks in ways that the original producers cannot determine and control."[16] The *Downfall* meme (which I discuss in depth in chapter 4), for example, includes thousands of "incorrectly" subtitled video parodies of the same four-minute scene from director Oliver Hirschbiegel's movie *Downfall* (2004).[17]

Burgess, calling on Jenkins's concepts of "participatory media" and "spreadable media," explains that when "viewed from the perspective of cultural participation rather than marketing," YouTube videos are neither "messages" nor "products," but in fact are the "mediating mechanisms [through] which cultural practices are originated, adopted and (sometimes) retained within social networks."[18] For YouTube users who "actively contribute content and engage in cultural conversation around online video," YouTube is not just a place to post and watch videos; it is a social network where videos "are the primary medium of social connection between participants."[19] Additionally, Henry Jenkins argues that the value of media, when used *as* (rather than *for*) social engagement, lies in its "spreadability," its capacity to be reused, reworked, and redistributed. Spreadable media become more culturally significant by "taking on new meanings, finding new audiences, attracting new markets, and generating new values."[20] An online video meme thus "produces cultural value to the extent that it acts as a hub for further creative activity by a wide range of participants in [a given] social network."[21]

ADAPTATION AND PERFORMANCE STUDIES

From a performance studies perspective, a "science of cultural transmission" (which is how Burgess describes memetics), is not the most useful way to analyze, explain, and address the implications of the internet video meme phenomenon. In performance terms, an internet video meme would be better described as an extensive series or collection of adaptations, which are inspired by one or multiple video source(s). Yet, the discipline of performance studies currently lacks a vocabulary to cogently analyze, clarify, discuss, and theorize the implications of these new forms of adaptation. According to literary theorist Linda Hutcheon, "most of the work done on [performance] adaptation has been carried out on cinematic transpositions of literature, but a broader theorizing seems warranted in the face of the phenomenon's variety and ubiquity."[22] Yet Hutcheon's own book, *A Theory of Adaptation,* barely scratches the surface in terms of looking at online adaptation. Meanwhile, referring to online adaptations as "memes" overlooks the crucial, creative, human component involved in the adaptive process. Thus, from a performance perspective, I prefer the term *adaptation* to meme. "Online meme" suggests that these videos are not just created *with* but also *by* the machine, the computer. Video memes, however, just like longer cinematic adaptations of literature (or vice versa), do not make and spread themselves. People make them, and people make them popular. These shorter adaptations are conceived and created out of an artistic impulse similar to the one that might drive someone to adapt literature for the stage or screen. The short length of an online video adaptation does not make it any less of an adaptation. Additionally, the lack of change in the type of mediation involved (i.e., video-to-video, rather than book-to-movie) does not disqualify the work from being viewed as an adaptation.

The key that connects "meme" to "adaptation" is that both refer to a performance that marks a change in some previous performance. As performance studies scholar Richard Schechner might say, these performances (memes, when viewed as *adaptations*) are a form of "restored behavior."[23] Following Schechner, David Román describes performance as an act that "stands in and of itself as an event; it is part of the process of production. A performance is not an entity that exists atemporally for the spectator; rather, the spectator intersects in a trajectory of continuous production."[24] Online video memes, like theatrical productions, are "composed of a series of performances."[25] Memes, as performances of adaptation and/or re-performances—even when they aim for fidelity toward their source—*always* change the original performance in some way. Román notes that all re-performances contain deviations, and this phenomenon is inherent in any restored behavior. Further, as Hutcheon states, "because adaptation is a form of repetition without replication, change is inevitable, even without any conscious updating or alteration of setting. And with change come corresponding modifications in the political valence and even the meaning of stories."[26] Focusing on the performances of adaptation that necessarily create what many refer to as internet memes allows one to consider how and why certain stories (and the various meanings of these stories) persist, or fall by the wayside, in our participatory media culture.

For this study, I define adaptation broadly, following Hutcheon's theories about adaptation and theatre and performance studies scholar Rebecca Schneider's theories about reenactment. In *A Theory of Adaptation*, Hutcheon studies adaptation as both a process and a product. To Hutcheon, adaptations are "deliberate, announced, and extended revisitations of prior works."[27] Hutcheon argues that while case studies often privilege the "source" or "original" text, "there are many and varied motives behind adaptation and few involve faithfulness [to some] original."[28] Hutcheon's book is not a study of specific examples or specific media, but instead looks to an array of media beyond the traditional novel-to-screen (or vice versa) adaptation. Rather than studying adaptation in terms of the media employed, Hutcheon uniquely considers adaptation as a process of transcoding stories to engage audiences. This process takes the form of three primary modes: telling (e.g., novels, short stories), showing (e.g., "all performance media"), and physically/kinesthetically interacting (e.g., videogames or theme park rides).[29]

Hutcheon posits that a variety of possible motives drive people to create adaptations, including (but not limited to) "the urge to consume and erase the memory of the adapted text or to call it into question [and] . . . the desire to pay tribute by copying."[30] Regardless of the adapter's motives, "adaptation is an act of appropriating or salvaging, and this is always a double process of [re]interpreting and then [re]creating something new."[31] With an adaptation, there is inevitably "difference as well as repetition."[32] Hutcheon points out that "part of this ongoing dialogue with the past, for that is what adaptation means for audiences, creates the doubled pleasure of the palimpsest: more than one text is experienced—and knowingly so."[33] Ultimately Hutcheon defines "adaptation" as "an acknowledged transposition of a recognizable other work or works," "a creative and an interpretive act of appropriation [or] salvaging," and "an extended intertextual engagement with the adapted work."[34]

Similarly, Rebecca Schneider defines reenactment as "repetition with revision," stating that repetition is always, "paradoxically, both the vehicle for sameness and the vehicle for difference or change."[35] Schneider argues that "any time-based art encounters its most interesting aspect in the fold: the double, the second, the clone, the uncanny, the againness of (re)enactment."[36] In this light, Schneider is interested in "reenactment as an activity that nets us all (reenacted, reenactor, original, copy, event, re-event, bypassed, and passer-by) in a knotty and porous relationship to time."[37] Schneider favors the term reenactment over "other terms for doubling that do not overtly accentuate time, such as mimesis, imitation, appropriation, citation, reiteration, [and] performativity."[38] Finally, Schneider discusses the so-called mistakes that occur in reenactments, and how these mistakes might be reframed not as failures, but as generative events. Schneider asks, "Is error necessarily failure? When is difference failure, and by what (geohistorical, chronopolitical) standard? And when, in the tracks of live acts, is a misquote or paraphrase a kind of revenant—getting it not so much wrong as getting it 'live' in a complex crosshatch of cross-affiliation?"[39] Reenactment, "a standard of oral history . . . does not link difference always already to failure and loss."[40]

PARODY AND POLYVOCALITY

Similar to Schneider's theories about reenactment, the *differences* in the adaptations I studied did not seem to focus on loss. More often than not, these differences seemed to have been added with the intention of being humorous; many of the videos were even overtly labeled as comedy or parody. Thus, I will also briefly explicate several theories that embrace the polyvocal qualities of parody. Mikhail Bakhtin, for instance, asserts that parodic texts date back to ancient history, and that these texts were just as relevant and respected as the texts they parodied. Parody was a natural inclusion in the life cycle of any text. Clark and Holquist, following Bakhtin, explain how the satyr play was the parodic "fourth drama" that followed a tragic trilogy, and used the same narrative and mythological motifs.[41] Parodic texts were not seen as profane or blasphemous, and authorship of these texts was proudly claimed. The purpose of a parody was to provide laughter and critique for existing straightforward genres and styles, allowing (or "forcing") the audience to experience multiple sides of a text.[42] Parodies, considered in this light, allow us to see the various forces at work in an "original" video, in terms of genre, style, and performance choices.

Hutcheon, meanwhile, theorizes that parody is a form of interpretation that asserts its producer's position in relation to the original text. Parody is always political, exposing power structures, cultural trends, and ideologies. Hutcheon further states that "parody is doubly coded in political terms: it both legitimizes and subverts that which it parodies."[43] Yet, while parody "may indeed be complicitous with the values it inscribes as well as subverts . . . the subversion is still there."[44] Parodies also inevitably include some change of context. According to Hutcheon, "[t]he contexts of creation and reception are material, public, and economic as much as they are cultural, personal, and aesthetic. This explains why, even in today's globalized world, major shifts in a story's context—that is, for example, in a national setting or time period—can change radically how the transposed story is interpreted, ideologically and literally."[45] Studying multiple parodies of the same video, in this sense, would reveal what narratives and ideologies are being maintained and/or subverted, and how people are using parody to achieve these ends.

Finally, performance artist Deb Margolin defines parody as "the direct result of an attempt to make room for oneself within an airtight, closed, or exclusive social, cultural, or theatrical construct"; as "a kind of aria of the poor," made with "the brashest and most heart-rending voice of the outsider looking in."[46] For the purposes of this study, I combine Bakhtin's and Hutcheon's theories with Margolin's powerful definition: "Parody" thus refers to the creative adaptation of a text that has explicitly changed the form and/or content of the source text, and in doing so acknowledges the complex set of forces at work in the adaptation. By adapting a text to celebrate and/or critique it, a parody asserts its producer's position in relation to said text.

Applying Hutcheon's ideas about adaptation (aside from the caveat that adaptations must be "extended engagements"), allows me to consider each video in this study as an intertextually engaged repetition without replication. Schneider's theory about re-enactment, as a sort of double-voiced repetition that complicates our sense of time and event, also allows me to consider videos that would otherwise be viewed as shot-for-shot remakes (i.e., *mere imitations*) as something more complex, as citations of previous texts through the embodiment of an Other—a new and different performer. Beyond just comparing these adaptations in terms of their fidelity to some original video, I consider what new bodies, voices, and performances bring to the video text, and subsequently to potential readings of the video by audiences who may or may not be familiar with the original. Hutcheon's consideration of adaptations in terms of mode (rather than medium) is also a unique and useful template from which to start my video analyses. However, the predominant types of videos I analyze do not fit so easily into Hutcheon's "showing" mode (which she applies to all performance media), and require different modes or trans-mode explanations. Thus, I have created a glossary of video-to-video adaptation methods (detailed below) to address this issue. Additionally, I employ a performance studies framework that allows me to consider the adaptations in this study as performance texts, as cultural and sociopolitical engagements, and further allows me to show how *doing* an adaptation is crucial to a deeper understanding of the processes and products of adaptation.

SIGNIFICANCE OF THE PERFORMANCE STUDIES FRAME

According to performance studies scholar Paul Edwards, "Adaptation has become an everyday art and a ubiquitous communication practice of digital consciousness, playing in improvisatory ways beyond the boundaries of the identified, sustained artwork."[47] As Edwards states, "no artist, group or community can lay claim to having invented adaptation as an art form."[48] Yet, performance studies has a long-standing relationship with adaptation. As a descendent of oral interpretation, the discipline of performance studies has extensive historical engagements with various methods of adapting non-dramatic texts into performances.

Performance studies scholars and artists are also arguably better at *doing* text adaptation, or at the very least, we create adaptations more often and more enthusiastically than scholars and artists in other academic disciplines. Robert Breen's chamber theatre, a form of literature-to-stage adaptation, for example, was first practiced in Oral Interpretation classes at Northwestern University beginning in the 1940s. In the book *Chamber Theatre,* Breen outlines a method of adapting literary works for the stage that uses a large portion of the work's original text, includes minimal theatrical illusion, and emphasizes the storyteller's point(s) of view "through physical representation onstage."[49] Breen's work influenced further performance adaptation practices, including feminist chamber theatre methods,[50] and was adopted (and adapted) as a method for staging literary texts in more traditional theatrical settings. In the essay, "'Novelizing' the Stage: Chamber Theatre After Breen and Bakhtin," for example, Michael Bowman identifies "some of the paradoxes or limitations of chamber theatre as a staging idiom,"[51] and uses Bakhtin's theory of the novel to suggest an alternate approach to chamber theatre. Meanwhile, chamber theater is only one method among many that performance studies scholars and artists have used to create performance adaptations of non-dramatic literature. Looking beyond these methods, into nonliterary forms of transmedia adaptation, it is not difficult to see that "adaptation is not a timeless theory or a set of techniques, but a succession of diverse embodied practices, driven by desire and even desperate neediness" to re-tell stories "in one's own time and place."[52] Calling on the "storytellers of Lookingglass [Theatre]," Paul Edwards additionally suggests that re-telling, "in one's own medium, in one's own time and place, is a kind of aesthetic transfusion."[53] Further, the act of retelling itself implies the questions "Why tell this story?" and "Why now?"[54]

The tradition of adaptation in performance studies continues today. Across the United States, performance studies classrooms and performance spaces often include a variety of intermedia adaptations, pulled from a diversity of sources (e.g., folk tales, encyclopedia entries, movie genres, ethnographies, contemporary fiction, social media, installation art, academic articles, dissertations, and so on). Dwindling resources and funding for many arts and humanities programs in higher education creates challenges, in terms of doing performance and text adaptation rather than merely teaching about it. Even so, more than a few Performance Studies programs still use adaptation as a creative practice/process in classrooms and public performances. Yet, despite this ongoing adaptation of adaptation practices, Edwards notes in "Adaptation: Two Theories" that we are largely at a loss for contemporary theories about adaptation and performance. The two most recent texts that discuss theories of adaptation are *A Theory of Adaptation* by Linda Hutcheon and *Adaptation and Appropriation* by Julie Sanders. While both books move beyond page-to-stage or page-to-screen adaptations, they don't move far beyond this, nor do they address noncommercial adaptation in any substantial way. Regarding these two books, Edwards "wonder[s] finally how well a focus on large-scale works in time-honored forms (opera production, published novels, feature films) serves a twenty-first-century theory of adaptation."[55]

Neither Hutcheon nor Sanders explicitly discuss internet memes or online video adaptations. Yet, as adaptation is very clearly—and quickly—spilling out of the traditional, culturally sanctioned spaces and texts that Hutcheon and Sanders *do* theorize about, there still has been little scholarly study of online adaptations as performance. Larger-scale studies about video memes and similar internet video trends, meanwhile, include the work of Jean Burgess, Joshua Green, and Henry Jenkins. While Burgess and Green's study of YouTube as a social networking site includes an analysis of user-generated/non-mainstream versus mainstream/corporate content, and a coding of various video types, they do not explicitly address online video adaptations or performance. Similarly, Henry Jenkins's studies of fan fiction (appropriating characters and settings of commercial works to create new content or expand upon the original story) do not explicitly consider how fan fiction works as adaptation or performance. Smaller-scale studies, meanwhile, include Rebekah

Willett's study of a single online video parody made by a group of young boys. Willett focuses on the relationship between commercial media texts and how young people form their identities, rather than on processes of adaptation or performance. David Gurney's study of textuality and participatory culture on YouTube similarly centers on only two appropriations of one viral video. Further, Gurney's notion of participatory culture is limited to the viewer comments, or "paratexts," that accompany the videos; Gurney does not consider the adaptations themselves as texts.

Meanwhile, though Hutcheon's *A Theory of Adaptation* is incredibly useful as a theoretical jumping-off point, the book is problematic in several ways when applied to online video adaptations. First, Hutcheon does not make a clear argument about the relation between parody and adaptation, at once citing parodies and adaptations as two distinct forms (e.g., "like parodies, adaptations have an overt and defining relationship to prior texts, usually revealingly called 'sources.' Unlike parodies, however, adaptations usually openly announce this relationship"[56]). Hutcheon also states, meanwhile, that "unlike plagiarism or even parody, adaptation usually signals its identity overtly: often for legal reasons, a work is openly announced to be 'based on' or 'adapted from' a specific prior work or works."[57] Later in the book, Hutcheon claims that "short intertextual allusions to other works or bits of sampled music" are not adaptations, but *parodies are*: "indeed parody is an ironic subset of adaptation, whether a change in medium is involved or not."[58] These claims are problematic not only because of the conflict in classification but also because many online video parodies *do* openly announce their relationship to some prior work. The *Downfall* parodies I discuss in chapter 4, for example, all use footage from an original feature film, and (seemingly in an attempt to protect themselves from lawsuits) many include a description stating that the producer of the parody does not own the copyright to the original film. Many of the video adaptations I discuss in chapters 2 and 3 also offer links to the original video in their video description, or have these links embedded into the video. The Gregory Brothers' "Bed Intruder Song," for example, includes a link to the original footage that the adaptation is based on, and a link that asks viewers to further adapt their music video, stating, "Post your version here!" This link takes users to a webpage where they can upload their own video adaptations of the "Bed Intruder Song."

Hutcheon also notes that "for economic reasons, adapters often rely on selecting works to adapt that are well known and that have proved popular over time; for legal reasons, they often choose works that are no longer copyrighted."[59] In the world of online video adaptation, economics are often not a factor in terms of what videos users choose to adapt, and "popularity over time" is less a factor than current popularity. Additionally, copyright issues are often acknowledged, but in a way that challenges these laws rather than conceding to them (as seen in the case of the

Downfall parodies and the "Streisand Effect," which I discuss in chapter 4). Hutcheon notes that technology and "new media" have "probably always framed, not to mention driven, adaptation,"[60] adding that "new electronic technologies have made what we might call fidelity to the imagination—rather than a more obvious fidelity to reality—possible in new ways, well beyond earlier animation techniques and special effects."[61] While this is certainly true in some cases, the practice of "sweding" cinema (which I discuss in depth in chapter 5) stands in contrast to this claim. Beyond a necessary video camera, sweding makes use of "old" technologies and requires a fidelity to the imagination—in terms of creatively using older technologies for special effects—just as much as a fidelity to the material reality of the very same technologies. Producers of sweded movies generally don't use newer electronic technologies in their creative process; they only use these "newer" technologies to make their low-tech videos widely available to anyone who wants to watch, and to watch the sweded videos that others have made.

Hutcheon draws on Dawkins's explanation of memes, as "units of cultural transmission or units of imitation," to explain how stories and ideas are adapted.[62] According to Dawkins, memes are "replicators" like genes. To adapt and survive in the "meme pool," memes change as they are transmitted, through processes of "continuous mutation" and "blending."[63] Hutcheon applies Dawkins's "list of the three qualities needed for high survival value," including longevity, fecundity, and copying-fidelity, to her theory of cultural adaptation, explaining that, like memes, stories evolve by adaptation through "cultural selection."[64] Stories "propagate themselves when they catch on; adaptations—as both repetition and variation—are their form of replication."[65] Hutcheon's use of the term "meme," now the word of choice to describe certain online adaptation trends, seems both obvious and fortuitous in retrospect. The first known cultural meme to make the jump to the internet, for example, was the "Internet Coke Machine" in 1982: A Coke machine at Carnegie Mellon University, which was connected to the internet so students could check if it was full. Yet, most of the major websites dedicated to researching, creating, and archiving internet memes did not pop up until after Hutcheon's *A Theory of Adaptation* was first published in 2006.[66] At the same time, in her exploration of "interactive electronic media," Hutcheon does not go beyond a discussion of video game adaptations, though online adaptations in a variety of media were around in the early 2000s. The omission is understandable, as the book was published only a year after the creation of YouTube. Today, however, this trend is no longer ignorable, as a multitude of new online video-to-video adaptations pop up every day, and many are "interactive," in the sense that they openly invite further adaptations or reference/engage additional popular internet adaptations. In the second edition of Hutcheon's book, Siobhan O'Flynn's added epilogue does discuss digital adaptation and transmedia storytelling. While this chapter expands Hutcheon's theory of adaptation to include the internet, it still deals mostly with "fan adaptations" of larger cultural works (e.g., the *Star Wars* series), digital adaptations of published books, and newer developments regarding adaptation theory and video games. Sweded videos are afforded a mention in this epilogue, but they are relegated to the status of "fan adaptation" with the "obvious goal" of replicating and adhering to "the model of a pre-existing work in the same medium."[67] To O'Flynn, sweding is "understood as engagement with and promotion of a prior project."[68] Yet, as I explain in chapter 5, the implications of sweded movies are much more complex (and less obvious) than simply "fan-adaptation" and film promotion.

Performance studies scholar Michael LeVan, following Paul Edwards, notes a lack of significant study of digital adaptations, and confirms that performance adaptation theory has been limited "mainly [to] traditional performance contexts."[69] LeVan quotes Edwards, pointing out that current adaptation theory "fails to map a large part of the terrain," including "practices of adaptations that utilize digital mediums like image, video, and sound—the practices of digital composition and recomposition that is at once medium, force, and content, and that often summons performance praxis into action."[70] In other words, the practices of digital composition like the online video-to-video adaptations I address in the following chapters exist within this "unmapped terrain." Edwards, meanwhile, describes "performance practice . . . as a 'democratized' practice of and for the multitude, and as an aesthetic practice blurring boundaries in the space of friction between performance object and performing subject."[71] LeVan suggests that we understand digital performance in a similar way: "As a multimodal and expansive indicator for what performance can be, how it can be accomplished, and where and when it can be enacted,"[72] and notes that "digital methods and contexts provide an opportunity to transform all areas of performance praxis."[73] Rather than studying the *act* of interpretation, LeVan suggests we consider "transformation as a concrete form," inclusive of "interpretation, adaptation, translation, transposition, interaction, and recombination" in and across multiple media.[74] Widely accessible, user-friendly, digital technologies coupled with online social networking rapidly breed this form of appropriation/transformation/adaptation. Adaptations can work online as play, performance, communication, cultural commentary, and/or dialogue. In social media contexts, Margolin's "aria of the poor" becomes polyphonic and contrapuntal. Contemporary theories of adaptation (like Hutcheon's) are useful, but fall short in this context. In other words, a larger-scale study of the more recent trends of everyday adaptation that transgresses and muddies the on/offline binary—a study that goes beyond analyzing just a few adaptations of a single, culturally sanctioned source text, in a traditional performance context—is quite overdue.

LeVan, meanwhile, also suggests a new model of performance in which we might "rethink notions of audience and of the stage," "orient our work to new distributions of performance space, performance time, and performance movement," and "rethink notions of event and encounter."[75] To build this model, some in-depth exploration of the performances in/of the "digital shoals" LeVan describes is a necessary first step. The following steps, after my in-depth exploration, include offering a glossary of strategies that allows for clear discussion of these phenomena, explicating and interpreting my findings, and drawing connections between existing theories (and histories) of performance, media studies, cultural studies and the newer types of performance adaptations I am studying. Additionally, I suggest further interdisciplinary research trajectories for the study of online adaptations (including adaptations using media I do not explicitly address in this study), which could benefit from a performance framework similar to the one used here.

GLOSSARY OF DIGITAL ADAPTATION STRATEGIES AND CHAPTER OUTLINE

According to media studies scholar Anders Fagerjord:

> Most videos on YouTube are people filming themselves. They put up a camera and talk to it, or perform in front of it, often in silly ways. Before video sites like YouTube, films of this kind were shared among friends and shown in the living room, if they were made at all. YouTube has provided a platform for people where they can share these performances with the whole wired world. Everyone can become a broadcaster. . . . Most people who take this opportunity use it to perform themselves or their selves, as previously noted.[76]

What I am interested in, however, is not just how people are performing themselves, but rather how people are performing others, or performing themselves through the performance of Other. To aid in this endeavor, I have created this glossary of online video-to-video adaptation strategies. While glossaries like this one can never be exhaustive, and there are always overlaps and exceptions to the rules, it still helps to have a working vocabulary to use when discussing newer video-making trends. The following glossary of strategies is thus meant to elucidate the terms I use in this book, which describe different methods of digital adaptation. They are listed here roughly in the order in which they will appear in chapters 2 through 5:

- Reenactment: Humans physically performing in videos, seemingly attempting to stay true to some "original" performance. No video editing software is involved, unless the software is necessary to reenact the prior edit. No overt or seemingly intentional aesthetic devices that differ from the original video. One example of a reenactment, which is discussed at length in chapters 2 and 3, would be a person videotaping himself re-performing a word-for-word section of a news interview, complete with gestures, tone of voice, and facial expressions that indicate attempted fidelity to the original interview.

- Remake: Involves some level of conscious choice on the part of the creator, in terms of fidelity (or lack thereof) to their "original" source video. Uses aesthetic devices, and/or includes video editing or manipulation of bodies that is intended to mimic editing techniques used in the original. For instance, a video of a person re-performing an *entire* news interview (rather than just a section), who plays both interviewer and interviewee in the video, would be a remake. The creator would have to use some sort of editing technique to cut between the news anchor and the person being interviewed. The creator may also take liberties, by adding/subtracting dialogue or using visual strategies, to call attention to specific parts of the interview. Rather than the impersonations found in reenactments, a remake might be composed of caricatures of the individuals being portrayed. Cartoons and animation can also be used to create remakes, and can themselves be remade.
- Remix: The label "remix" comes from the music world. However, similar processes have been used in a variety of other creative arts, e.g., literary cut-ups. Here, I use the term remix to refer to videos that fragment and recombine pieces of some "original" to make something new. Remixes rearrange, combine, and/or recontextualize fragments of the original, and offer an alternate version of the text. Remixing can be compared to John Hartley's description of the process of "redaction," or "the production of new material by the process of editing existing content."[77] As video remixes do not simply re-perform the original text like remakes do, remixes are also less likely to reveal their producers, physically. Because they interpret and alter the original text, remixes also offer a wide range of explicit and implicit cultural commentary, from the celebratory to the incendiary. In chapter 3, I offer examples of remixes of the news interview of a woman named Sweet Brown. These remixes use her image and voice, along with other videos and voices, to create performance adaptations that have transformed the original interview into another form and/or context, like a rap battle, gospel song, or a video that creates the illusion that Sweet Brown is having a conversation with some person who was not in the "original" video.
- Response: These videos include vlog responses and video parodies that depart overtly and drastically from the content and/or context of the original video. Response videos offer some sort of cultural commentary; their creators offer a clear perspective on the sociocul-

tural issue(s) at hand or on the original video. As a very loose form of adaptation, response videos can also work to extend the shelf life of a given video meme, without necessarily re-performing any of the original video at all. In chapter 3, for example, I discuss a vlog that was created as a direct response to Sweet Brown's news interview, along with other parodies that use Sweet Brown's "character," but remove her from the original interview context. In chapter 4, meanwhile, I discuss an interview with actor Bruno Ganz which was "creatively subtitled" (definition below), to appear as if Ganz was responding to a popular video adaptation trend that uses his likeness.

- Songification: Songification, a term I borrow from the musicians The Gregory Brothers, involves scavenging through existent video footage for "accidental singers," people who speak with passionate pitch variation and whose voices have a natural musical quality.[78] To songify a video, the vocal track is filtered through an autotune vocorder—a device that disguises singers' off-key inaccuracies and creates perfectly tuned vocal tracks. Autotuning the speaking voices of these "accidental singers" produces song-like results. To complete the songification process, the autotuned footage is cut and remixed to create a structured song, generally with verses and a chorus. The Gregory Brothers became famous through their use of songification. Their YouTube series "Autotune the News," for example, used a variety of news sources to create new songs. In chapter 2, I discuss The Gregory Brothers' popular "Bed Intruder Song" (2010), which is a songified version of a newscast about an attempted rape in Huntsville, Alabama.
- Cover: Covering is a type of homage. With the spirit of the jazz musician, another performer re-performs the "silent" score of a work, and inevitably adds something unique in their re-performance. "My version of . . . " videos generally fall here. Additionally, covers may or may not be musical. For example, a video that might otherwise be considered a reenactment or remake but contains some indication of non-parodic personalization on the creator's part would constitute a cover, even if no music were involved. As The Gregory Brothers became popular on YouTube, for example, they began to post links accompanying their videos, asking audiences to "Post Your Version Here!" The link would take users to The Gregory Brothers website, where they could upload a capella versions of the "Bed Intruder Song," or perhaps versions of the song using electric guitars, drums, accordions, acoustic guitars, pianos, flutes, and other physical and digital musical instruments and technologies.
- Techno-play: Videos in which it seems that, more than anything else, the producer was trying their hand at, playing with, and/or

learning how to use the technologies they are working with. In chapter 3, I discuss remakes of a news interview that use excessive amounts of video editing for no clear or obvious reason as a form of techno-play. In chapter 4, I discuss how YouTube users teach each other how to create subtitles for videos through unique, performative, instructional videos as techno-play. Finally, sweding, which I discuss in chapter 5, can be a form of techno-play, based on how much experience the creator has with film technologies.

- Creative subtitling: The process of creative subtitling works through intentionally inaccurate (and often humorous) language translation. The translator works in the realms of non-verbal expression, affect, and cinematography—in everything *but* the literal words. Tone of voice, facial expressions, kinesics, proxemics, haptics, the physical appearance of the onscreen characters, and cinematographic choices are interpreted and translated by the creative subtitler. In chapter 4, for example, I focus on a number of videos that have "incorrectly" subtitled the same scene from the movie *Downfall,* to make some personal, social, or cultural statement that usually has little or nothing to do with the movie *Downfall.*
- Sweding: The terms "sweding" and "sweded," which are inspired by Michael Gondry's 2008 film *Be Kind Rewind,*[79] refer to re-creations of Hollywood movies that use limited resources and poor, "bad," or cheap technology. Sweded movies are *much* shorter than the original movie, usually falling within the 2-to-8-minute range. Rather than spend millions of dollars to make a movie, sweders work on a shoestring budget to craft props and special effects, and create music to mimic/remake some "original" movie. In *Be Kind Rewind,* for example, the lead characters use little money, and create costumes, sounds, and special effects for a number of Hollywood movies, including *Ghostbusters, The Lion King, Rush Hour 2, Driving Miss Daisy,* and *Robocop,* among others.

In this book, I mark distinctions between these nine methods of online video adaptation. There is overlap among the categories, but the distinctions still aid in my consideration of the implicit and explicit cultural commentary that various video adaptations might be making. Re-performance will always be different from the original performance in some way—i.e., repetition *with revision*—though this revision may be mostly or entirely unintentional. For example, a reenactment might seem to be as straightforward as a "remake" that aims for mimesis (i.e., shot-for-shot movie remakes, impersonations, and imitations). These texts seem to be re-performed with no intentional changes made to the text. As the creators of these types of video remakes re-perform, they seem to offer little to no explicit cultural commentary that deviates from the original. Yet, as Hutcheon states, "remakes are invariably adaptations because of changes in context,"[80] and these changes can alter the potential meaning(s) of the text.

Chapters 2 and 3 focus on adaptations of local news footage segments which quickly became viral videos/internet memes, and how the meanings of these videos change through new performances. In these chapters, I look specifically at the videos "Antoine Dodson Warns a PERP on LIVE TV!!!"[81] and "Sweet Brown: No Time for Bronchitis."[82] The widespread adaptation of both of these news segments indicates that both videos have significant cultural implications. The adaptations of these two videos also map a complicated relation between traditional news media, representations of black Americans on television, the replication of historically problematic scripts, and the possibilities that YouTube offers in terms of the proliferation and/or subversion of these scripts. In chapter 2, I concentrate on Antoine Dodson video adaptations, and in chapter 3 I address Sweet Brown adaptations and their relation to the Antoine Dodson videos. Through both chapters, I draw historical connections between contemporary video adaptation trends on YouTube, representations of black Americans in popular culture, traditions of minstrelsy, musical adaptation, camp, and children's culture, to explain that the ways people have adapted—and are still adapting—the Dodson and Brown videos both challenge and re-inscribe dominant stereotypes and ideologies. These two videos demonstrate how the adaptation trends of any single video can be varied, complex, and unpredictable. The adaptations of these two videos also bring up a smorgasbord of social, cultural, and ethical issues, particularly in terms of the performance of an Other, and performances that use class, race, and gender stereotyping.

Chapter 4 focuses on the process of creative subtitling, and the performative nature of the *Downfall* (or "Hitler Reacts to . . . ") video meme. Using close readings and comparative analysis, I show how adapters use the movie *Downfall,* along with other *Downfall* parodies, as models for further creative acts, personal expression, and cultural commentary. Additionally, I offer the *Downfall* meme as one example of how online video adapters have been successful in terms of rebelling against and creatively navigating archaic copyright laws. Finally, I use *Downfall* adaptations to exemplify how these types of performances of adaptation can be socially complex ways of reworking the context (rather than the content) of a video, to make personal, social, or cultural statements.

Cultural historian and film critic Leo Braudy explains that film remakes work because of "unfinished cultural business" or the "continuing historical relevance (economic, cultural, psychological) of a particular narrative."[83] I expand Braudy's notion of narrative to include not only the narrative in the film, but also other relevant sociopolitical narratives that could influence the process and product of the remade film. Sweded movies, which I discuss in chapter 5, can be viewed as a type of remake. At the same time, sweded movies are often funny not because the original movie was funny, but because the processes and products of sweding lampoon the big-budget movie industry and highlight the ridiculousness of traditional, expected Hollywood aesthetics. The terms "sweded" and "sweding" describe the process of remaking short versions of popular movies on a shoestring budget, creatively using what is at hand. Producers of sweded movies do not always use digital technologies to make their videos, yet they bridge the off/online binary by using digital media and online social networking to disseminate their low-tech videos, and to watch the sweded movies others have made. Taking a hands-on performance approach, chapter 5 interweaves several threads, including a (nonexhaustive) historical precedence for sweded cinema, descriptions and analyses of some popular sweded videos, and a personal account of the process of sweding the movie *Dirty Harry*. I explain how sweded cinema, as a form of adaptation, is not unique to the digital age or digital technology, and also how sweded cinema thrives when performers and audiences are equally invested in the creation and appreciation of "bad" or "amateur" art. Sweded movies are at once "bad" art for art's sake, a lampoon of big-budget Hollywood filmmaking norms, and often a highly social endeavor.

To limit the scope of this book, the videos I selected to watch were all shared through YouTube, Google Video,[84] and websites specifically dedicated to sweded cinema and the *Downfall* meme. I looked at websites dedicated to sweded cinema and *Downfall* because they are trusty places to find larger collections of these videos, and they offer a web community to their users that is smaller in scope than most video-sharing sites. I looked at YouTube because it is the online platform where all of the video adaptation trends I am studying were initially shared.[85] YouTube is also one of the largest and most popular online video-sharing communities in the world, and is the top site in the United States for user-generated video.[86] Finally, while Google Video searches resulted in overlap with YouTube, these searches occasionally offered links to other video sites.

Additionally, I do not make a distinction between *amateur* and *professional* videos in this book. To do so would be nearly impossible, as these terms have, at best, ambiguous meanings in video-sharing communities. While the meanings of these words are by no means transparent, many people still use them as if they are. In doing so, we "repeat implicitly, and without sufficient critical distance, the premises of the American commercial theatre,"[87] where professional performance is equivalent to paid performance. According to performance and media studies scholar Nick Salvato, "[t]he moment we begin to examine activity that happens outside this narrowly circumscribed field, we see how inadequately the economic distinction between amateur and professional fits other modes and models of performance."[88] The quality of many noncommercial videos, for example, fits professional standards. Further, making a clear distinction between noncommercial and commercial videos is tricky, as You-

Tube, for instance, offers partnership deals and monetization opportunities to some of its users, and advertises on other users' videos without compensating them financially. I have thus only included videos that have no *obvious* financial intentions, though it is possible that some of the videos I discuss have been monetized by their creators. Finally, this book is by no means a comprehensive overview of online video-to-video adaptation trends. Rather, I focus on several significant types of adaptations and adaptive processes, with specific examples, to help us navigate the ever-growing archive of online performances of adaptation. I am thus posting *my* version *here*, of what personal, social, cultural, historical, and legal sense we might make of these performance phenomena. I begin, in chapter 2, with a case study of the now (in)famous Antoine Dodson and "The Bed Intruder" adaptations, which peaked in late 2010, and continue to pop up from time to time in 2017.

NOTES

1. Jamie Dubs, "Downfall/Hitler Reacts," Know Your Meme, Cheezburger Inc., accessed July 18, 2012, http://knowyourmeme.com/memes/downfall-hitler-reacts.
2. Dubs, "Downfall/Hitler Reacts."
3. Dubs, "Downfall/Hitler Reacts."
4. Katerina Clark and Michael Holquist, *Mikhail Bakhtin* (Cambridge: Belknap-Harvard University Press, 1984), 276.
5. Henry Jenkins, *Convergence Culture: Where Old and New Media Collide* (New York: New York University Press, 2006), 290.
6. Jenkins, *Convergence,* 257.
7. John Fiske, *Reading the Popular* (London: Routledge, 1989), 1.
8. Fiske, *Reading,* 2.
9. John Fiske, *Television Culture* (Padstow: T J Press, 1987), 117.
10. Fiske, *Reading,* 6.
11. Fiske, *Reading,* 117.
12. Fiske, *Reading,* 108.
13. Fiske, *Reading,* 117.
14. Richard Dawkins, *The Selfish Gene* (Oxford: Oxford University Press, 1976).
15. Jean Burgess, "'All Your Chocolate Rain Are Belong to Us'? Viral Video, YouTube and the Dynamics of Participatory Culture," in *The Video Vortex Reader,* eds. Geert Lovink et al. (Amsterdam: Institute of Network Cultures, 2008), 1.
16. Burgess, "All Your Chocolate Rain," 1.
17. *Downfall,* dir. Oliver Hirschbiegel, perf. Bruno Ganz, Constantine Films, 2004.
18. Burgess, "All Your Chocolate Rain," 2.
19. Burgess, "All Your Chocolate Rain," 2.
20. Henry Jenkins, "'Slash Me, Mash Me, Spread Me . . . ,'" *Confessions of an Aca/Fan,* April 24, 2007, accessed August 1, 2012, http://henryjenkins.org/2007/04/slash_me_mash_me_but_please_sp.html.
21. Burgess, "All Your Chocolate Rain," 2.
22. Linda Hutcheon, *A Theory of Adaptation* (London: Routledge, 2012), Kindle edition, loc. 111.
23. Richard Schechner, *Between Theatre and Anthropology* (Philadelphia: University of Pennsylvania Press, 1985).
24. David Román, *Acts of Intervention: Performance, Gay Culture, and AIDS* (Bloomington: Indiana University Press, 1998), xvii.

25. Román, *Acts of Intervention*, xvii.
26. Hutcheon, *Adaptation*, loc. 187.
27. Hutcheon, *Adaptation*, loc. 139.
28. Hutcheon, *Adaptation*, loc. 139.
29. Hutcheon, *Adaptation*, loc. 139.
30. Hutcheon, *Adaptation*, loc. 326.
31. Hutcheon, *Adaptation*, loc. 563.
32. Hutcheon, *Adaptation*, loc. 2206.
33. Hutcheon, *Adaptation*, loc. 2239.
34. Hutcheon, *Adaptation*, loc. 353.
35. Rebecca Schneider, *Performing Remains: Art and War in Times of Theatrical Reenactment* (New York: Routledge, 2011), Kindle edition, loc. 381.
36. Schneider, *Performing Remains*, loc. 281.
37. Schneider, *Performing Remains*, loc. 372.
38. Schneider, *Performing Remains*, loc. 886.
39. Schneider, *Performing Remains*, loc. 1132.
40. Schneider, *Performing Remains*, loc. 1140.
41. Clark and Holquist, *Mikhail Bakhtin*, 54.
42. Clark and Holquist, *Mikhail Bakhtin*, 59.
43. Linda Hutcheon, *The Politics of Postmodernism* (New York: Routledge, 1989), 101.
44. Hutcheon, *Politics*, 106.
45. Hutcheon, *Adaptation*, loc. 704.
46. Deb Margolin, "A Performer's Notes on Parody," *Theatre Topics* 13.2 (2003): 248.
47. Paul Edwards, "Adaptation: Two Theories," *Text and Performance Quarterly* 27.4 (2007): 375.
48. Paul Edwards, "Staging Paradox: The Local Art of Adaptation," in *SAGE Handbook of Performance Studies*, eds. D. Soyini Madison and Judith Hamera (Thousand Oaks: Sage, 2006), 227.
49. Robert S. Breen, *Chamber Theatre* (Evanston, IL: Wm. Caxton, 1986), 4.
50. For instance, Laura Diekmann's "Towards a Feminist Chamber Theatre Method" (1999), in which Diekmann discusses the construction of a feminist chamber theatre method based on Breen's model of adaptation.
51. Michael Bowman, "'Novelizing' the Stage: Chamber Theatre After Breen and Bakhtin," *Text and Performance Quarterly* 15.1 (1995): 1.
52. Edwards, "Staging Paradox," 233–34.
53. Edwards, "Staging Paradox," 247.
54. Edwards, "Staging Paradox," 242.
55. Edwards, "Adaptation," 375.
56. Hutcheon, *Adaptation*, loc. 261.
57. Hutcheon, *Adaptation*, loc. 2328.
58. Hutcheon, *Adaptation*, loc. 3144.
59. Hutcheon, *Adaptation*, loc. 3144.
60. Hutcheon, *Adaptation*, loc. 3144.
61. Hutcheon, *Adaptation*, loc. 3144.
62. Hutcheon, *Adaptation*, loc. 775.
63. Dawkins, *The Selfish Gene*, 195.
64. Hutcheon, *Adaptation*, loc. 3286.
65. Hutcheon, *Adaptation*, loc. 3286.
66. For example, Reddit (2005), Cheezburger (2007), KnowYourMeme (2008), and FailBlog (2008). And while 4chan (2003) has been integral to the creation and dissemination of many internet memes, this site was initially created for and used by a smaller subculture of anime fans.
67. Siobhan O'Flynn, "Epilogue," in Linda Hutcheon's *A Theory of Adaptation* (London: Routledge, 2012), Kindle edition, loc. 3751.
68. O'Flynn, loc. 3751.

69. Michael LeVan, "The Digital Shoals: On Becoming and Sensation in Performance," *Text and Performance Quarterly* 32.3 (2012): 219.
70. LeVan, "The Digital Shoals," 219.
71. Paul Edwards, as quoted in LeVan, "The Digital Shoals," 219.
72. LeVan, "The Digital Shoals," 213.
73. LeVan, "The Digital Shoals," 218.
74. LeVan, "The Digital Shoals," 218.
75. LeVan, "The Digital Shoals," 218.
76. Anders Fagerjord, "After Convergence: YouTube and Remix Culture," in *International Handbook of Internet Research,* eds. J. Hunsinger et al. (New York: Springer Science + Business Media, 2010), 197.
77. John Hartley, *Television Truths: Forms of Knowledge in Popular Culture* (London: Blackwell, 2008), 112.
78. Stefan Sirucek, "ATTI: Auto Tune the Interview," July 6 2010, *The Huffington Post,* accessed March 23, 2011, http://www.huffingtonpost.com/stefan-sirucek/atti-auto-tune-the-interv_b_649113.html.
79. *Be Kind Rewind,* dir. Michel Gondry, perf. Jack Black, Mos Def, New Line Cinema, 2008.
80. Hutcheon, *Adaptation,* loc. 3151.
81. Crazy Laugh Action, "Antoine Dodson Warns a PERP on LIVE TV!!! (Original)," YouTube, July 29, 2010, accessed Sept. 21, 2013. (Video has been removed from YouTube and re-uploaded by Crazy Laugh Action as "ANTOINE DODSON - FUNNIEST NEWS INTERVIEW EVER (Original)," YouTube, April 11, 2012, accessed Sept. 5, 2016, https://www.youtube.com/watch?v=EzNhaLUT520.)
82. Lucasmarr, "Sweet Brown: No Time for Bronchitis," YouTube, Apr. 9, 2012, accessed July 18, 2012, https://www.youtube.com/watch?v=JaAd8OuwwPk.
83. Leo Braudy, "Afterword: Rethinking Remakes," in *Play It Again, Sam: Retakes on Remakes,* eds. Andrew Horton and Stuart Y. McDougal (Berkeley: University of California Press, 1998), 331.
84. The videos on Google Video were (for the most part) moved to YouTube in 2011, when the website shut down, according to "Google Video (Archive)," accessed Oct. 21, 2016, http://www.archiveteam.org/index.php?title=Google_Video_(Archive).
85. Including the first "How to Swede" video, the first creative *Downfall* subtitle, the Antoine Dodson news footage, and the Sweet Brown news footage.
86. According to YouTube's "Statistics" page in March, 2014, "100 hours of video are uploaded to [the site] every minute" and "over 6 billion hours of video are watched each month."
87. Nick Salvato, "Out of Hand: YouTube Amateurs and Professionals," *The Drama Review* 53.3 (2009): 69.
88. Salvato, "Out of Hand," 69.

TWO

The Many Voices of Antoine Dodson

On July 29, 2010, NBC affiliate WAFF-48 aired a live news story about an attempted rape in Huntsville, Alabama. The story included an interview with claimant Kelly Dodson, who curtly told the reporter that she "was attacked by some idiot from out here in the projects."[1] Following this, the story focuses on Kelly's brother, Antoine Dodson (as seen in figure 2.1). We learn that Dodson heard his sister scream, rushed into her bedroom, and saw the accused perpetrator escape through a window. In the interview, Dodson warns viewers about potential public danger, stating, "Well, *obviously* we have a rapist in Lincoln Park. He's climbing in your windows; he's snatching your people up, trying to rape 'em. So y'all need to hide your kids, hide your wife, and hide your husbands, cuz they rapin' everybody out here."[2] Waving a rolled-up paper at the news camera, Dodson belittles the accused perpetrator, stating, "We got your t-shirt, you done left fingerprints and all. You are *so* dumb. You are really dumb. For real. . . . You don't have to come and confess that you did it. We're looking for you. We, we *gon' find* you, I'm letting you know *now*. So you can run and tell *that*, homeboy."[3]

YouTube user Crazy Laugh Action uploaded the Dodson news video onto YouTube several hours after the live news airing, and the video quickly went viral. Later that night YouTube users began to upload their own versions of the Dodson video, adaptations that included many videos emphasizing Dodson's impassioned interview. One of the earliest adaptations of the Dodson video, the "Bed Intruder Song" by The Gregory Brothers, was cited by YouTube as the most viewed viral video of 2010. The "Bed Intruder Song" also made it onto the Billboard Hot 100 in August 2010. As Jenna Worthrom of the *New York Times* states, the song was "one of the stranger twists in recent pop-music history . . . [and] a rare case of a product of Web culture jumping the species barrier and

Figure 2.1. Screenshot of "Antoine Dodson Warns a PERP on LIVE TV!!!"
***Source*: Screenshot courtesy of WAFF-48.**

becoming a pop hit."[4] The Gregory Brothers' hit was ranked on the Hot 100 among singles by Usher and Katy Perry—two very popular and well known musical artists in 2010. Meanwhile, YouTube users were remaking, remixing, and parodying the "Bed Intruder Song" en masse—in part because The Gregory Brothers posted the chords and lyrics online and encouraged others to "create their own version of the song."[5]

On April 7, 2012, just as Antoine Dodson was beginning to recede into distant internet meme memory, Sweet Brown (pictured in figure 2.2) inadvertently invoked his likeness. A fire broke out at Brown's apartment complex in Oklahoma City, leaving one person hospitalized for smoke inhalation and damaging five apartments. KFOR News Channel 4 interviewed Brown, one of the residents who lost her apartment. During the interview Brown explains, "Well, I woke up to get me a *cold pop*, and then I thought somebody was *barbecuing*. Then I said, 'Oh Lord *Jesus*, it's a *fire*!' Then I ran out, I didn't grab no *shoes* or nothing, Jesus! I *ran* for my life! And then the smoke *got me*. I got *bronchitis*! Ain't nobody got time for that!"[6]

KFOR employee Ted Malave uploaded the Sweet Brown news clip to YouTube on the same day, but another version (uploaded by lucasmarr on April 9, 2012) is the most shared version to date, having gained "over 1 million views and over 109,000 Facebook shares within [the first] 48 hours."[7]

Figure 2.2. Screenshot of "Sweet Brown: No Time for Bronchitis."
***Source*: Screenshot courtesy of KFOR News Channel 4.**

Parallels between the Antoine Dodson and Sweet Brown news videos were immediately apparent to a number of news writers, bloggers, and video creators, many of whom referred to Brown as "the next Antoine Dodson."[8] As one blogger wrote about the Dodson meme, "Part of the Dodson meme is, I fear, about laughing at mannerisms that the mainstream associates with blackness, gayness and poverty. There is nothing amusing about a young woman assaulted in her home. And so, I worry that people are laughing at Antoine: his flamboyance and perceived gayness; his use of black colloquialisms, like 'run tell dat,' his grammar and accent."[9] There is also nothing funny about an apartment fire. Yet, like Dodson, Brown's news interview went viral, and many people found the video to be humorous. Brown's headscarf and passionate delivery bring to mind Dodson's interview. Beyond this, her mannerisms, language choice, and accent also invoke similar stereotypes that are associated with blackness and poverty:

> It's her bright head scarf. It's the gold teeth that keep flashing as she speaks. It's the way she unabashedly calls on her god. It's the way she says Lord Jesus, it's faahr! in a drawl that speaks of the backwoods. It's her emotionalism. It's her very name: Sweet Brown. . . . Sweet Brown is so country. So poor. So uneducated. So (stereotypically) black. For most video watchers, so other. And that makes her not a recipient of sympathy, but ridicule.[10]

While this explanation, laughter at someone who is "so other," may be true for some video watchers, the widespread adaptation of both the Dodson and Sweet Brown news footage indicates more complicated relations between the news clips and their many viewers. YouTube users have been inspired to adapt these videos in various ways, including creating video remakes, remixes, reenactments, covers, and response videos, which suggests that the Dodson and Brown news videos have significant cultural implications. Through their adaptations of Antoine Dodson and Sweet Brown's news interviews, video-makers are making a place for themselves on YouTube and also making social and cultural statements. While other viral videos are widely adapted, the adaptations of these two videos map a complicated relation between news media, representations of black Americans on television, the replication of historically problematic scripts, and the possibilities that YouTube offers in terms of the proliferation and/or subversion of these scripts.

Following Henry Jenkins's notion of participatory culture, I am interested in YouTube users who do something with these two viral videos beyond watching and forwarding. These spectators-turned-producers adapt the viral video in some way to create a new video, and in doing so, they grow the video meme, both perpetuating and subverting racial, gender, and class stereotypes. In this chapter, I concentrate on Antoine Dodson video adaptations, and in chapter 3 I address Sweet Brown video adaptations and their relation to the Antoine Dodson meme. Through both chapters, I draw historical connections between contemporary video adaptation trends on YouTube and representations of black Americans in popular culture, traditions of minstrelsy, musical adaptation, camp, and children's culture, to explain how people have adapted—and are *still* adapting—the Dodson and Brown videos both challenge and re-inscribe stereotypes and ideologies.[11]

Close readings of the video adaptations, along with an analysis of the similarities and differences among these videos, can provide "valuable clues to the readings that a particular culture or subculture is likely to produce."[12] John Fiske theorizes that while the meaning of a text can be hard to pin down, we might address this by "shift[ing] our focus from the text to its moments of reading."[13] In other words, studying how people are adapting (and by extension "reading") the Dodson video within specific social and historical constructs would prove more fruitful than analyzing the Dodson video on its own, to determine its possible meanings. Also, trends among the adaptation of a single base text should reveal larger underlying values and power structures that are being propagated or challenged. Thus, through close readings and comparative analysis of over 200 Antoine Dodson video adaptations and over 200 Sweet Brown video adaptations, I consider the adaptations in terms of their vertical intertextuality, or their relation to the original news interviews, and their horizontal intertextuality, or potential relations to each other.[14] Of course, viral videos and their adaptations make cultural statements with varying degrees of power and efficacy, and my interpretations of what cultural commentary the videos might be making on their own and/or in relation to each other are undoubtedly affected by my own experiences and personal subjectivity. At the same time, taking note of common trends and motifs among the videos (particularly specific attempts at reproducing or changing the original visual or spoken performance) reveals on a larger scale how people are interpreting and "using" the Antoine Dodson and Sweet Brown videos, regardless of what I interpret the adaptations to be implicitly or explicitly saying.

My process to determine which video adaptations to analyze included YouTube searches of "Antoine Dodson Parody," "Antoine Dodson Remake," and "Antoine Dodson Remix." I chose these phrases because they brought up videos that were relevant to Antoine Dodson, but generally left out news, interviews, and other television appearances Dodson made after his original news interview went viral. Of these results, I analyzed the top 50 that YouTube offered when sorted by most relevant.[15] I then re-sorted the videos on YouTube and analyzed the top 50 most recent, top 50 most viewed, and top 50 highest rated. I wanted to select a sample of videos that would be most representative of the videos others might watch if they conducted the same search. By re-sorting the videos, I allowed for variety in terms of what people who were looking for adaptations of the Dodson footage would be most interested in watching (relevant videos, newer videos, or popular videos). Overall, the trends in my findings (in terms of patterns among the Dodson adaptations I studied) were consistent for each of the four sorting methods. This process was completed over several months in early 2011 and then repeated in early 2013. My method in deciding which Sweet Brown adaptations to watch paralleled how I chose the Dodson adaptations.[16] I conducted YouTube searches of "Sweet Brown Parody," "Sweet Brown Remake," and "Sweet Brown Remix," and watched the top 50, sorted in terms of most relevant, most recent, most viewed, and highest rated. These searches took place between October 2012 and July 2013. When analyzing the videos, I was not *looking* for anything in particular, aesthetically. I attempted to remain open to what each of the videos uniquely offered. I took note of the visual, verbal, and tonal elements of the video that the creator changed or reenacted as well as the social or cultural statements the creator might be intentionally or unintentionally making with the video. Finally, I fit many of the adaptations into the glossary of strategies outlined in chapter 1.

DODSON ADAPTATIONS: SONGIFIED OR OTHERWISE ALTERED

Viral video adaptations offer a unique way to study cultural trends because of the time factor involved in their creation and dissemination. It is common for adaptations of viral videos to start popping up the same day as the original video, sometimes within hours, and this was the case with the Antoine Dodson news video. (The "original" Dodson video was the most viewed News/Politics video on YouTube in 2010.) The most popular Dodson adaptation in late 2010, meanwhile, was the Gregory Brothers "Bed Intruder Song," a remix of the Dodson video that quickly became more popular than the original news footage. "Bed Intruder Song" has over 133 million views on YouTube to date.[17] The Gregory Brothers uploaded their musical remix of the Dodson video onto YouTube only two days after the original video aired, as part of their popular "Autotune the News" video series. The brothers create "Auto Tune the News" videos through a process they call "songification." To songify a video, they scavenge through current news footage for interesting stories and "accidental singers," or people who speak with passionate pitch variation and whose voices have a natural musical quality.[18] Next, they filter the audio of the selected news footage through an autotune vocorder, a device that disguises singers' off-key inaccuracies and creates perfectly tuned vocal tracks. Auto tuning the speaking voices of "accidental singers" produces song-like results. To complete the process, they cut and remix the songified news footage to create a structured song with verses and a chorus. With Dodson's permission, the Gregory Brothers songified Dodson's voice, remixed the original news footage, and spliced in several shots of themselves singing, to create the "Bed Intruder Song" and music video.

According to John Fiske, popular culture made from television news footage must be made *out of*, not *by* the news. In line with this, the Dodson video was not uploaded to YouTube by its original broadcasting source. According to Fiske, news texts will also only be made popular if they offer meanings relevant to subordinate people.[19] This implies that the Dodson news footage contains ideologies, messages, and/or performances that were relevant to current social power structures. Popular culture texts also offer space for excesses in adaptation, like "parody, subversion [and] inversion."[20] These excessive forms of performance make statements and create new meanings beyond those that might be inferred from the original text and can also communicate their producer's position within and beliefs about existing power structures. The Dodson news video lends itself to these excessive performances in a variety of ways, especially in terms of stereotypical performances of race, socioeconomic class, and gender. In the original video, a white news reporter is interviewing a black family (Antoine and Kelly Dodson). At the time of the interview, the Dodsons were poor; according to Kelly Dodson, they lived "in the projects."[21] Antoine Dodson is assumed to be a man by the news interviewers (i.e., during the interview he is referred to as "the victim's brother"). Yet his gender performance in the interview is mixed, as he combines traditionally masculine speech patterns (straightforward, dominant, attention-commanding, and controlling language) with conventionally feminine vocal and physical performances (verbose and emotional). Since 2010, academic and popular conversations in the United States about gender performance and fluidity have become increasingly open and complex. At the time of the Dodson news interview, however, his mixed gender performance was the most often parodied, mocked, and/or celebrated aspect of his "character" that creators incorporated into their adaptations.

While non-musical Dodson video adaptations vary widely in terms of type, aesthetic, style, subject, and tone, details performers often focus on or parody include Dodson's voice, emotionalism, effeminacy, and his over-the-top vigilante-ism. Meanwhile, there were notable differences in terms of how men and women adapted Dodson's interview.[22] Many remakes, for example, feature men attempting to exaggerate the femininity of Dodson's performance. The men—more often than the women—changed (i.e., *raised)* the pitch of their voice, over-performed Dodson's already exaggerated emotions, and used body positioning and movement that could be thought of as stereotypically feminine (e.g., wiping real or imaginary hair out of their eyes, standing with one hip cocked and one or both hands on their hips, etc.). Men also changed the specific wording and context of the interview more often than women—placing Dodson in other locations and dealing with different crimes.

Whether these performances were intended to celebrate, mock, or otherwise comment on Dodson's hybridized gender performance is often unclear. Regardless of the performers' intentions, however, most of these videos work on multiple levels, as their creators seem to be simultaneously making fun of and *having fun* exploring traditional gender stereotypes. The women that perform in Dodson reenactments and remakes, meanwhile, seem to be more openly celebrating Dodson's comfort with his own gender hybridization. These women keep Dodson's dialogue, generally word for word, stressing how Dodson simultaneously expressed his physical femininity along with his traditionally (active, powerful, attention-commanding) masculine message, "You don't have to come and confess that you did it. We're looking for you. We, we gon' find you, I'm letting you know now. So you can run and tell that, homeboy."[23]

Some producers changed the alleged crime—attempted rape—to address other issues. Others appropriated Dodson's character into different contexts. These alternate crimes and contexts included car accidents, ninja attacks, robberies, a variety of Christmas themed videos, a fraternity party, Michael Jackson's "Thriller" music video, and a workout video. Some videos parodied social networking sites ("Facebook Intruder"), popular television shows like "The Office," and popular movies like *Black Swan*. Recent events that the Dodson video adaptations address included global issues (e.g., "Tsunami Intruder," a video about the tsunami waves that hit Japan and Hawaii on March 11, 2011), national issues (e.g., "Fed intruder," which mocks the 2011 US administration and liberal politicians), and local issues (e.g., "MHS Principal Intruder," made for a performance event at a Cleveland, OH high school).

POINTS OF CONVERGENCE: RACE, CLASS, AND GENDER PERFORMANCE

According to bell hooks, "We are all so accustomed to looking solely from the standpoint of sex or race or class that the overlaps, the mergers, the place where nothing is as clear as it would seem are often ignored."[24] Yet, the most common motifs among the Dodson video adaptations included racial and class stereotypes, and these often occurred simultaneously. Many parodies (regardless of the producer's race) exaggerated the number and types of things the perpetrator left on the scene. These additional things the perpetrator left behind were often objects that indicated he was lower class and (stereotypically) black. In addition to the t-shirt that Dodson mentions in the original video, adaptations included items left behind like fried chicken, watermelon, and teeth (e.g., because "nobody around here got all their teeth"[25]). When I imagine crime-scene evidence, fried chicken is generally not something that comes to mind. Yet, a number of videos mention this food item that is stereotypically associated with black Americans.

One such video remake even changed the crime from rape to "a woman who woke up to a stranger, trying to steal fried chicken from her." A younger Asian American man plays all of the roles in the video, changing his costume and make-up accordingly. He splices in one image from the original news footage, showing an aerial map of Dodson's neighborhood, and states (as the news anchor), "The break-in happened this morning, somewhere in the middle of a hood, where we don't really care about." As Kelly Dodson, he wears a wig and bright make-up, and claims, "Don't nobody try to steal my chicken!" Finally, as Dodson, he warns the viewing public to "Hide your Kool-Aid, hide your cornbread, and hide your watermelon, cuz he eatin' up e'rythang!"[26]

Another video stars an older black woman, a younger black woman, and a younger black man. (Both young performers in the video appear to be in their early teens.) They all speak with obviously affected African accents, and wear animal print togas and head-wraps. The older woman holds a rolled up paper (à la Dodson's newspaper) while the young man wields a giant machete and the young woman holds a wooden spear. The young woman plays Dodson, stating, "We have a rapist in the jungle. He tried to rape my brother." The women share the following information about what the perpetrator left, stating, "We have evidence. You left behind your bucket of chicken. We know you are from the projects. You left KFC. You left your Nike shoe. We know you are an American from the American projects. . . . You left your alcohol bottle empty. . . . You left your generic polo shirt we know you buy from the Chinese corner store in your projects."[27] This explanation points to the video's creators' assumptions about the assumed race and class of the perpetrator and his astonishing ignorance, reinforcing stereotypes about the projects, the (black, lower class) people who live there, and how they behave.

A "country" version of the Dodson interview, meanwhile, changes the location of the crime to "Lincoln Trailer Park," to focus only on socioeconomic status, rather than race.[28] A young white woman initially plays Dodson; she is dressed like Dodson, and incorporates some of his quotes. She starts to tell the story, but breaks into tears early in the video, and asks a white man—her father—to take over. She disappears from the video, and the father tells the story of the attempted rape, changing a few details to make stereotypical comments about trailer parks, and the (white, lower class) people who live there, all while waving a beer bottle at the camera (rather than a newspaper).

RESPONSE VIDEOS AND CAMP

Following Susan Sontag's essay, "Notes on Camp," Camp can be defined as a strategy of reading that sees the world in terms of aesthetics and style: "the essence of Camp is its love of the unnatural: of artifice and exaggeration."[29] Camp is an ironic and parodic appreciation of a form that exceeds its content. For Sontag, pure Camp is naive and unintentional, "exhibiting a failed seriousness and/or passionate ambition."[30] In "Camp and the Gay Sensibility," Jack Babuscio elaborates on four basic features of Camp: irony, aestheticism, theatricality, and humor. Camp irony is "any highly incongruous contrast between an individual or thing and its context or association."[31] Camp aestheticism is "style as a means of self-projection, a conveyor of meaning and an expression of emotional tone."[32] Camp humor, meanwhile, attempts to reconcile conflicting emotions: it is "a means of dealing with a hostile environment and, in the process, of defining a positive identity."[33] Babuscio also argues that "Camp humor relies on an involvement, strongly identifying with a situation or object while comically appreciating its contradictions. In this it is different from the detachment that facilitates mockery."[34]

One campy Dodson video adaptation removed the attempted rape from the story, seemingly in attempt to address racial and class stereotyping more directly. The video stars an older white man wearing a canary yellow suit and checkered tie, along with a panama hat. He sits in a rocking chair in front of a fireplace. His home looks fancy, overdone with ornate tchotchkes lining the mantle. As he waves his glass of rosé champagne, he states: "*Obviously*, we have a black man intruding here on the grounds of the Hamptons. *Obviously*, the black man doesn't hold a degree from an Ivy League institution of higher learning. He left fried chicken bones and watermelon rinds in the pool. Why would a black man be in a swimming pool? Everyone knows they can't swim." The man laughs evilly, then continues: "Perhaps he was there to clean the pool."[35] He has named his character, in the video's title, "Antoine Dodson, the Rich White Racist." This blatant self-labeling as racist along with the evil laughter and overdone set and costuming seems to suggest that rather than supporting racial stereotypes, this man is attempting to use aspects of camp humor in his character and dialogue to subvert these stereotypes, by calling attention to their absurdity.

Another video, which is also in line with Babuscio's features of camp, addresses the use of celebrity, commercialism, performance, and self-degradation for money. In the video made by YouTube user BarrettTV, titled "Antoine Dodson discusses his new show based on Bed Intruder," a black man plays Dodson and a black woman plays Kelly.[36] They stand outside of an apartment complex, which has obviously been green-screened in, as the video begins with a remake of the news footage. The man incorporates many of Dodson's quotes, while Kelly says nothing and then quickly disappears from the frame. The man states, "I know my sister almost got raped, and that was great 'cause now I'm a celebrity and everybody loves me."[37] He goes on, "I'm making a lot of money and we moved out of the projects, so that's real nice." He then announces that he's "going on the road" with his sidekick Antoinette Dodson. Antoinette, played by the same woman who played Kelly, appears in the frame. She is dressed exactly like Dodson, and they recite the famous Dodson quotes together in a robotic fashion. Then the "Bed Intruder Song" begins to play, and they start lip-syncing and dancing, as if they are making an impromptu music video. The robotic way they perform the song makes them look like puppets—they even do the robot dance.

According to Rebecca Schneider, "the potential aspect of camp at the undecidable edges of sincerity is deeply important. . . . For, as in camp performance generally, that which is gotten slightly wrong in the effort to get something right, is precisely the space where difference is unleashed as critical homage."[38] The puppet-like performances in this video create an atmosphere of empty entertainment for financial profit. The two perform a very scripted and predictable Antoine and Antoinette, showing that they are critical of entertainers like Dodson who seek financial profit by exploiting a near-tragic event. At the same time, the video uses Dodson as an example to comment on the larger "cewebrity" culture of monetizing internet fame, implicating the viewer as well as the cewebrity.

Further, According to Chuck Kleinhans:

> Camp is a strategy for makers as well as for reception. It draws on and transforms mass culture. In this it critiques the dominant culture, but in the dominant culture's own terms; it seldom rests on any coherent or sustained analysis of society or history. Camp always uses parody but, more importantly, it embodies parody as a general mode of discourse. As a mode of discourse, parody typically operates within the dominant ideology, but with an internal tension. Since Camp is an especially

> acute ideological form containing active contradictions it can, in certain social and historical contexts, challenge dominant culture.[39]

Kleinhans uses the example of the cakewalk, "a processional dance originating in the antebellum plantation American south," to show how parody does not reside in the work alone but is derived from the stance(s) people take toward the work.[40] The cakewalk was a show in which black slaves were given "cast-off clothing, finery unsuitable for their ordinary labor, and thus dressed up proceeded to parade (often with a cake as the prize, hence the name of the dance)."[41] Slave masters were amused by the "inappropriate" clothing and extreme gestures the slaves performed, "as if they had the refined manners of aristocrats." However, "for the slaves who participated, and hateful as this scorn might have been, it was also an opportunity to mock the masters' manners."[42] The cakewalk influenced future performance genres, including the minstrel show. Kleinhans further states:

> From the visual evidence we have forty years later, preserved in the first silent films, we can see how blacks parodied the whites' fancy manners in a comic form that safely contained, but certainly did not eliminate, social criticism. On one level the stage representation contributed to the racist myth of the happy plantation and, on the other, it revealed the persistence of a critique within popular forms. Whites remained amused and superior, but blacks could read the subversive ridicule involved. Everyone laughed, but one side laughed differently from the other.[43]

BarrettTV's video adaptation, described above, includes performances that show Dodson being empowered by his newfound cewebrity. At the same time, this empowerment is contingent upon the endless repetition of a single news interview and popular song, both of which make Dodson look foolish. Additionally, rape is addressed as a potentially positive impetus. Here, the attempted rape of Kelly Dodson set into motion the possibility of Antoine's rise to fame and fortune. Kelly was almost raped, but because she wasn't, Antoine can unselfconsciously take center stage as the performer of the family, the saving grace that allows them to escape the projects and move on to a better life.

LOSS IN TRANSLATION: FROM NEWS TO SONG

The most skimmed-over, changed, or omitted element in many of the Dodson video adaptations is the attempted rape. Many producers changed the word *rape* to *take*, especially covers and remakes of the "Bed Intruder Song" performed by younger people and choirs. Liberty Choir's a cappella group, for example, covered the "Bed Intruder Song" for their Christmas concert, using the original tune and lyrics, only changing the word "rape" to "take." The reason for this change, according to the choir conductor, was that they did not want to offend any rape survivors that might be in their audience. This indicates that the choir did acknowledge how a pop song about attempted rape might be problematic in a fun, holiday context. Yet, the choir then performed a version of Carol of the Bells, using Dodson's phrases "You are so dumb," "You can run and tell that, homeboy," and "You are really, really dumb," as lyrics.[44] While possibly entertaining to some audiences, this version of Carol of the Bells explicitly negates the context of Dodson's statements in favor of a cheery, festive, silliness.

Another video, featuring comedian Donnell Rawlings, changes the issue of attempted rape of Kelly Dodson to a homophobic response video supposedly made by the perpetrator (played by Rawlings). In Rawlings's parody of the "Bed Intruder Song," a censor bar intentionally ineffectively conceals the perpetrator's identity as he addresses his audience (assumedly Dodson), accusing Dodson himself of being a rapist, "tranny," "homo," and "queer."[45] There is no indication that Rawlings's musical response is meant to offer anything beyond blatant homophobia as attempted humor. Elijah G. Ward, meanwhile, posits that "[t]heologically-driven homophobia, aided by black nationalist ideology, supports a strong and exaggerated sense of masculinity within black communities that, along with homophobia, takes a significant but generally unexamined psychic and social toll on the lives of . . . black gay/bisexual men [and] black heterosexual males and females."[46] Rawlings's "comedic" video does little beyond perpetuating this culture of hypermasculinity and homophobia. Following E. Patrick Johnson's theory of appropriation, Amber Johnson argues that "social media users frame Dodson's identity as coonery, which appropriates gay, black masculinity in limiting ways."[47] While Johnson studies only three videos and their responses to determine this, Rawlings video could be easily added to her list. Yet, there are hundreds of other YouTube performances of Antoine Dodson (some of which I discuss above) that work to reframe his identity in different ways and/or challenge the blatant homophobia in videos like the one Rawlings stars in.

SONGIFICATION AND OPERATIC IDEALS

Philip Kennicott of the *New York Times*, meanwhile, compares the "Bed Intruder Song" to Italian opera, pointing out that for centuries, people have wondered why the Italians were opera's first, most enthusiastic, and most successful advocates. Kennicott explains that the issue is one of language. One observer in 1785, for example, wrote that Italian "seems full of interjections, of exclamations, of distinct and perceptible tones." Music historian Charles Burney wrote in 1789, "Every dialect has peculiar inflexions of voice, which form a kind of tune in its utterance."[48] The theory was that spoken Italian was already halfway to music, and all Italian composers had to do was coax it along to create opera. The condescension toward the Italians in this view is not much of a stretch from the idea that African Americans are "naturally musical." However, over the centuries, composers seeking to introduce new national forms of opera have consistently looked to inflection and rhythmic patterns in speech for hints on how to compose their melodies.

Kennicott posits that we might call the "Bed Intruder Song" fundamentally operatic. The Gregory Brothers have uncannily mimicked the contours of Dodson's speech. Like many arias, the song captures a moment of intense emotion. However, as Kennicott points out, if this were part of an opera by Handel, there would be some contrasting emotional element. According to Kennicott, in the hands of an eighteenth-century composer, the missing element in the "Bed Intruder Song" would perhaps express "Dodson's happy memories of a time when his neighborhood was safer, or tender concern for his sister's wellbeing. Something that would make Antoine Dodson a more fully dimensional character."[49] Autotuned news footage is fundamentally different from opera in another important way: In opera, the characters are not appropriated from everyday life; "the wonderful, raving lunatics of 18th-century opera—the crazy Roman emperors, petty tyrants, and jealous barbarian warlords—had been dead for centuries or were invented altogether."[50] These "characters" couldn't just hop onto YouTube one day, only to find themselves caricatured, singing in a voice not quite their own.

Throughout the history of opera, there has been a recurring debate about whether the ideal should be "first the music, then the words" or the opposite. Many great composers believed in "first the words, then the music." "First the words, then the music" has also generally been a call in opera to return to a focus on real people, real emotion, and real depth—as opposed to florid songs, extremes of expression, or wild stage business.[51] Autotuning, remixing, or otherwise adapting television news footage and turning it into a song—another form of "first the words, then the music"—is the technological realization of this old operatic dream, but it is at the loss of something elemental: the actual human empathy that makes us *care about* what the people are singing. Even if it's scary or tragic—like rape. Or fire.

NOTES

1. Crazy Laugh Action, "Antoine Dodson Warns a PERP on LIVE TV!!! (Original)," YouTube, July 29, 2010, accessed Sept. 21, 2013. (Video has been removed from YouTube and re-uploaded by Crazy Laugh Action as "ANTOINE DODSON—FUNNIEST NEWS INTERVIEW EVER (Original)," YouTube, April 11, 2012, accessed Sept. 5, 2016, https://www.youtube.com/watch?v=EzNhaLUT520.
2. Crazy Laugh Action, "Antoine Dodson Warns a PERP."

3. Crazy Laugh Action, "Antoine Dodson Warns a PERP."
4. Jenna Worthrom, "From Viral Video to Billboard 100," *The New York Times*, Sept. 5, 2010.
5. Worthrom, "From Viral Video."
6. lucasmarr, "Sweet Brown: No Time for Bronchitis," YouTube, Apr. 9, 2012, accessed July 18, 2012, https://www.youtube.com/watch?v=JaAd8OuwwPk.
7. ColtonW, "Sweet Brown / Ain't Nobody Got Time for That," *Know Your Meme*, accessed Sept. 5, 2016, http://knowyourmeme.com/memes/sweet-brown-aint-nobody-got-time-for-that.
8. For example, Tammi Winfrey Harris, "Move Over, Antoine Dodson! The Ironically Racist Internet Presents Sweet Brown," *Clutch Magazine*, Apr. 10, 2012; Charlieville, "Sweet Brown: The New Antoine Dodson," *Break*, Apr. 11, 2012; Gabe Delahaye, "Sweet Brown Is OUR Generation's Antoine Dodson," *Videogum*, Apr. 11, 2012.
9. Tammi Winfrey Harris, "What's So Funny About Antoine Dodson?" *Change.org News*, Aug. 24, 2010, accessed Aug. 1, 2012.
10. Harris, "Move Over."
11. In this chapter, I focus on how internet users have adapted the Antoine Dodson news footage and not on how Dodson performed his own identities. For a discussion of the way Antoine Dodson performed his own intersectional identities for the news interview, along with the positive impacts that Dodson's interview performance (and how he chose to capitalize on his unexpected fame) had on his own life and the lives of others, see: Amber Johnson, "Antoine Dodson and the (Mis)Appropriation of the Homo Coon: An Intersectional Approach to the Performative Possibilities of Social Media," *Critical Studies in Media Communication* 30.2 (2013): 1–19.
12. John Fiske, *Television Culture* (Padstow: T J Press, 1987), 108.
13. Fiske, *Television*, 117.
14. Fiske, *Television*, 117.
15. YouTube's default sorting method in 2013.
16. An earlier version of this chapter was published as the multimedia essay: Lyndsay Michalik, "How Antoine Dodson and the Bed Intruder Keep Climbin' in Our Windows: Viral Video Appropriation as Performance," *Liminalities: A Journal of Performance Studies* 10.3/4 (2014), http://liminalities.net/10-3/index.html.
17. As of Sept. 5, 2016.
18. Stefan Sirucek, "ATTI: Auto Tune the Interview," July 6, 2010, *The Huffington Post*, accessed March 23, 2011, http://www.huffingtonpost.com/stefan-sirucek/atti-auto-tune-the-interv_b_649113.html.
19. John Fiske, *Reading the Popular* (London: Routledge, 1989), 3.
20. Fiske, *Reading*, 6.
21. Crazy Laugh Action, "Antoine Dodson Warns a PERP."
22. Gender as declared on YouTube, at the time of the creator's video upload.
23. Crazy Laugh Action, "Antoine Dodson Warns a PERP."
24. bell hooks, *Reel to Real* (New York: Routledge, 1996), 121.
25. JamJamBigLow, "Woman Wakes Up to Find Intruder in Her Bed (Antoine Dodson Spoof)," YouTube, July 31, 2010, accessed March 22, 2011. (Video has been removed from YouTube.)
26. ShortFunnyAsian, "Antoine Dodson—Woman Wakes Up to Find Intruder in Her Bed (PARODY)," YouTube, Aug. 4, 2010, accessed June 22, 2012. (Video has been removed from YouTube.)
27. luvvyheart, "Antoine Dodson African Parody," YouTube, Aug. 12, 2010, accessed Mar. 22, 2011. (Video has been removed from YouTube.)
28. McAlisterMania, "BED INTRUDER Antoine Dodson: Country Version," YouTube, Aug. 1, 2010, accessed Mar. 23, 2011. (Video has been removed from YouTube.)
29. Susan Sontag, as quoted in Chuck Kleinhans, "Taking Out the Trash: Camp and the politics of parody," in *The Politics and Poetics of Camp*, ed. Moe Myer (London: Routledge, 1994), 105.
30. Sontag, as quoted in Kleinhans, "Taking Out the Trash," 160.

31. Jack Babuscio, "Camp and the Gay Sensibility," in *Gays and Film,* ed. Richard Dyer (New York: Zoetrope, 1984), 41.
32. Babuscio, "Camp," 43.
33. Babuscio, "Camp," 47.
34. Kleinhans, "Taking Out The Trash," 161.
35. Oshacueru, "ANTOINE DODSON THE RICH WHITE RACIST," YouTube, Aug. 4, 2010, accessed Mar. 22, 2011. (Video has been removed from YouTube.)
36. BarrettTV, "Antoine Dodson Discusses His New Show Based on Bed Intruder," YouTube, Aug. 27, 2010, accessed Mar. 31, 2011, https://www.youtube.com/watch?v=pC0naK49Pb8.
37. BarrettTV, "Antoine Dodson."
38. Rebecca Schneider, *Performing Remains: Art and War in Times of Theatrical Reenactment* (New York: Routledge, 2011), 112.
39. Kleinhans, "Taking Out the Trash," 162.
40. Kleinhans, "Taking Out the Trash," 171.
41. Kleinhans, "Taking Out the Trash," 171.
42. Kleinhans, "Taking Out the Trash," 170.
43. Kleinhans, "Taking Out the Trash," 171.
44. Liberty University, "Bed Intruder Christmas Carol Song-Liberty University (LU) 2010 Christmas Coffeehouse," YouTube, Dec. 13, 2010, accessed Sept. 5, 2016, https://www.youtube.com/watch?v=RMB10wwmWrU.
45. djheat, "Donnell Rawlings aka Ashy Larry—Bed Intruder Response Song," YouTube, Aug. 31, 2010, accessed Sept. 19, 2013, https://www.youtube.com/watch?v=hXjBIu1GPm8.
46. Elijah G. Ward, "Homophobia, Hypermasculinity and the US Black Church," *Culture, Health & Sexuality* 7.5 (2005): 494.
47. Johnson, "Antoine Dodson and the (Mis)Appropriation," 5.
48. Charles Burney, as quoted in Philip Kennicott, "Auto-Tune Turns the Operatic Ideal into a Shoddy Joke," *The Washington Post*, Aug. 29, 2010, accessed Sept. 19, 2013, http://www.washingtonpost.com/wp-dyn/content/article/2010/08/27/AR2010082702197.html.
49. Kennicott, "Auto-Tune Turns the Operatic Ideal."
50. Kennicott, "Auto-Tune Turns the Operatic Ideal."
51. Kennicott, "Auto-Tune Turns the Operatic Ideal."

THREE

The Many Faces of Sweet Brown

The Sweet Brown news video has also been widely adapted, though not to the extent that the Dodson video has been. With Dodson, the song-making process seemed to be more like, first, the ridiculous musical voice (the "accidental singer"), then the words, then the music, then the invitation from the Gregory Brothers, Dodson, and many others to make your own version. The phrase "Post your version here!" is often embedded into musical Dodson adaptations, inviting covers and variations from viewers. Yet, the popularity of the "Bed Intruder Song" seems to have limited the creative musical response of many Dodson adapters, who, while they may change the lyrics, characters, and context, almost always use a version of the Gregory Brother's tune.

The "Bed Intruder Song" set a quirky precedent for autotune remixes of news footage. While there was no single huge autotune hit for Sweet Brown like there was for Dodson, several of the early popular adaptations of the Sweet Brown video *were* autotuned remixes, focusing the lines, "Ain't nobody got time for that!" and "I got bronchitis!" The most viewed Sweet Brown remix on YouTube in late 2013, for example, was an autotuned version that uses a catchy and repetitive tune and includes many video clips and images from sources other than the original interview. These include videos of people dancing, monkeys dancing, church services, images of Jesus, and even a photoshopped image of Antoine Dodson barbequing with Don King.[1]

The second most viewed Sweet Brown remix[2] is another catchy techno song, though this one is not autotuned. The song synchronizes Brown's speaking voice with the beat of the music. In the video description, the creators refer to the song as "Sweet Brown's new rap remix," though Brown had no part in the creation of the song. Rather, her voice was sampled and remixed to a beat. Other remixes change the speed of

Brown's voice. One uses the beat from Chris Brown's "Look At Me Now"; Another combines "God Don't Need No Matches" by the Mississippi Mass Choir, featuring Reverend James Moore, with Sweet Brown's voice. Some of these remixes are accompanied by carefully edited music videos, which are often remixes of other pop culture videos, church service videos, people singing and dancing, and/or images relevant to information in Brown's interview, including images of soda cans, barbecue, fires, Jesus, shoes, and smoke.

The lack of a "Bed Intruder"-like hit leaves more room for musical creativity for Sweet Brown musical adaptations. Indeed, there was more musical variation with the Sweet Brown news clip, than there was with Dodson. Numerous jazz versions sampled Sweet Brown's voice, or gave the interview text a new voice altogether. According to Dietmar Offenhuber, "jazz sets emphasis on performance, or the 'voice,' as opposed to the score. Its main principle is improvisation through a dialogic process between musicians."[3] The adapters that made jazz versions, in line with this, seem to see themselves as Brown's co-creators, rather than musical thieves or derivative samplers. In one jazz cover, "Sweet Brown Quartet," a man sings the lyrics, "When I felt the heat y'all, I ran for my life. . . . Wasn't no time for my flip flops, I ran for my life."[4] This man creates a dialogue between himself and Sweet Brown, combining the interview text, a sample of Brown's voice layered over his own, and his own musical composition. Another song, "SWEET BROWN COLD POP INSPIRATIONAL REMIX by Rodney Oliver Banks," relates Brown's story, in Banks's words, to a new tune. Banks describes the song, at the beginning of his video, as "the Cold Pop Remix by Sweet Brown, remixed by myself here, Rodney Oliver Banks."[5] Banks then performs this remix of a remix, including emphatic clapping, wild gesturing, and exaggerated facial expressions, from the acoustic sanctuary that is his shower. In his video description, Banks states, "When the spirit of a COLD POP, comes UPON MY HEART . . . I will RUN FOR MY LIFE!!! Bump SHOES!!! Ain't NOBODY GOT TIME FUH DAT!!!"[6]

LABELING, COVERS, AND CARICATURE: CONFUSION

Many mislabeled or multi-labeled Sweet Brown adaptations indicate that adapters aren't always sure what it is they are creating. A bible study youth group from the Church of God in Christ mass choir created a video "twist to Sweet Brown's 'Oh Lord Jesus, It's a FIRE (Ain't Nobody Got Time For That).'"[7] The title of their video is telling; it is a "twist," because they are not really covering or remixing anything. They are improvising on a theme, to a beat they are creating themselves with their bodies and voices, in the moment. They look like they are performing for each other, rather than an internet audience. The video looks as if a seemingly spontaneous performance was taking place in a public place (a parking lot or lawn of some sort), and someone nearby (perhaps another choir member) just happened to have a video camera.

Another example of labeling confusion is StatusMusicDesign's "Ain't Nobody Got Time For That (Less Than 1 min. Acoustic . . . Parody?)." The ellipsis and question mark in the title indicate his genre confusion. This acoustic guitar cover of one of the more popular Sweet Brown musical remixes sounds a bit like a 1980s hard rock ballad, and is described as follows:

> My friends and I cracked up for days about the Autotuned version of Sweet Brown's interview. Killed us. So I made this to make them laugh. . . . This is the world we live in: A woman makes some comments about a fire in her apartment complex. Someone autotunes it into a song. Some guy in Maryland makes a rough estimate of the chords/melody in said Autotune version and does an acoustic cover. MUSIC. Enjoy or not. Save the hatred . . . AIN'T NOBODY GOT TIME FOR THAT![8]

This *is* the world we live in; one where people make acoustic covers of autotuned news footage. However, this world is arguably not much different from worlds and times gone by. While the technology people use is newer, the instinct to remake/reuse/cover/perform one's own version of an existing work is not new. The white man who performs in the video described above claims he is just making a cover version of a song, and asks his audience to set aside their concerns about cultural or racial sensitivity. At the very least, he is requesting that this sensitivity take a back seat to the enjoyment of music, creativity, and his urge to add another voice to the polyphony of video adaptations—with or without intentional change or fidelity to the original news video.

Compared to the relatively homogenous music that was inspired by Antoine Dodson's news interview, covers and jazz songs created from Sweet Brown's news interview might be compared to the popular "coon song" of the late nineteenth and early twentieth century. The coon song's defining characteristic was its caricature of African Americans as "watermelon-and-chicken-loving rural buffoon[s]."[9] At the height of the coon song craze, "just about every songwriter in the country" was writing coon songs "to fill the seemingly insatiable demand."[10] Yet, according to Yuval Taylor and Jake Austen, in their book *Darkest America: Black Minstrelsy from Slavery to Hip-Hop,* racist music like the coon song should also be considered in context, as black artists "weren't just performing straight versions of these songs, like the white folks were. . . . [T]hey were jazzing them up. . . . [And] by jazzing up songs, performers present them with a wink and a shrug."[11] Similarly, jazzed up musical variations on the theme of Sweet Brown abound. And there is nothing inherently racist in the lyrics of many of the Sweet Brown musical adaptations. Meanwhile, her energetic physical and vocal performances seem to have inspired many of these adaptations, some which come off as caricatures of Brown.

Taylor and Austen discuss "the alchemy of spectatorship," stating that "the weight of the burden of stereotypes shifts dramatically when the white gaze is removed from black audience productions."[12] Citing an excerpt of a Bert Williams performance that was used for two different documentaries, Taylor and Austen note how the same footage can be used for markedly different purposes. The authors state, "[W]ithout whites watching, sometimes a funny eye bulge is just a funny eye bulge."[13] Similarly, Taylor and Austen quote Bill Cosby as stating, "In the confines of my own home I might say [in dialect voice] 'Yeah, Brutha Andy,' we might do the so forth and the so on. But we don't want the white people laughing at it."[14] The question for YouTube users, then, becomes: Are we ready for white, male, solo guitar players to adapt Sweet Brown into a song, with a wink and a shrug? Who is allowed to laugh, or to enjoy this version of the song? And according to whom?

TECHNO-PLAY AND EMBODIMENT

Many video adaptations made by younger creators, again, seem to focus on play and experimentation with technology, video composition, and genre. One group of young people used Sweet Brown's interview to complete a class assignment in storyboarding, editing, and video advertising. The only things the students kept from the original interview were the phrase "cold pop," and the character of Sweet Brown. Their video description states, "filmed by Mount St. Mary media students for a class assignment, this commercial follows Sweet Brown as she goes looking for a 'Cold Pop.'"[15]

Another video, created by two teenage girls, includes 33 seconds of reenactment and over twelve minutes of bloopers. The girls seem to be trying to get Brown's words exactly right. They also seem to be perfectionistic in terms of making this video exactly as they imagined; it just takes them a while to get there. By including bloopers, rather than just the "final product," they let their YouTube audience see their process. Thus, it seems as if they want their efforts to be acknowledged–that it took longer than 33 seconds to create their video, and they had a lot of fun making it. Further, even their bloopers are edited. They did not just leave the camera rolling and then upload everything to YouTube. They put their final product first, and then included an edited version of their process.[16]

Another group of young women made a music video to a songified version of the Sweet Brown interview, using many types of video edits, transitions, and special effects. Though they employ video editing software, their technique is far from masterful. The women seem to be learning different editing techniques as they figure out how to stage and cut the different scenes in the music video.[17] The group seems to have put a lot of technological and physical work into their final video. In addition to editing, for example, they perform many of the dances that were in the video they are remaking, imitating *The Fresh Prince of Bel-Air*'s "Carlton" dance, Janet Jackson's dancing, and a group of dancing monkeys with their own bodies. The women correspond their dances, nearly shot-for-shot, with where these dances occur in the original video. Thus, while the video is not very "good," in terms of conventional music video standards, their efforts seem great. Additionally, through the entire video they look like they are having fun.

A third group of young women create a remake of the music video of one of the Sweet Brown remixes, titled "Sweet Brown ('Ain't Nobody Got Time for That' Remix)," also using a combination of embodiment and technology.[18] This group uses video editing techniques, but they also use their bodies to imitate the editing in the original music video. For example, Brown's dance-like head turns were created through video cuts in the music video they are remaking. The girls create these "cuts" using only the movement of their bodies, by quickly turning their heads back and forth to the beat of the song.[19] Brown's technologically created "dance" becomes a *physical* dance, in their version of the music video.

SWEET BROWN REMAKES

Many of the Sweet Brown video adaptations that would qualify as remakes either aim for some sort of fidelity toward or parody of the original news interview. Parodied aspects include, like with the Antoine Dodson remakes, Brown's voice, physical performance, facial expressions, and emotionality. As with the Dodson meme, many Sweet Brown parodies riff on stereotypically black and/or lower class speech patterns and language use. Some videos are visually reminiscent of Dodson, as the performers dress up as Dodson, in a black shirt and red bandana, though they are performing as Brown in the video. Other parodies exaggerate what the performer doesn't have time for (i.e., "Ain't nobody got time for that!"). One man, for example, explains:

> So I was runnin', I was runnin' down the street and I seen that dog that's always knockin' over my garbage can on trash day, I said I'm gonna get that dog, so I walked over to the dog and the dog started growlin'. The dog got rabies! I got a weak immune system! Ain't nobody got time for that! So I ran the other way, Jesus, I sashayed down to my friendgirl's house, to use her phone to call the ambulam. She was cookin' greens. Greens give me gas! Ain't nobody got time for that![20]

Another performer made a video solely about the things he does not have time for. These things include donating money to a charity, supporting Newt Gingrich, getting another juice box, helping a child with homework, and taking out the garbage. After finishing his juice box, for example, the man exclaims, "Now I gotta get another one? Ain't nobody got time for that!"[21]

With Dodson, video adapters exaggerated the material things left at the crime scene. With Brown, adapters often exaggerate the amount of "irrelevant" information that Brown gives during her interview. In one video, a white man in a blond wig, "Sparkle Johnson," performs gender, class, and racial stereotypes through affected dialect, facial expressions, choice of words, and exaggerated outrage. Sparkle Johnson states:

> I ran for my life! I didn't even wake up my sister cuz I said, whatever, that bitch is high yella, she thinks she's better than everybody, she always pisses me off. I said fuck that bitch! Let her burn! And I couldn't call the fire department cuz I didn't pay my phone bill either. Jesus, sho nuf did not, okay? So I ran next door to the neighbor house and I'm banging on the door. I said, Shatrice! Shatrice! Shatrice! Call the muthafuckin *ambalance*! The fire department, uh, because the buildin' on fire! And this bitch *gon' ax me* what happen to the VCR she had leant me a couple days ago to watch a porno wit my man. I said, bitch, I ain't got time to talk about no mothafuckin' VCR you leant me so I could watch a porno! You know, the building's on fire, come on now, call the *ambalance*![22]

One thing the above-mentioned performers lack is the "background walker," who shows up in many other Sweet Brown video adaptations. In the news video, there is a man walking back and forth behind Brown, glancing at her and putting his hands to his face as she speaks. Many videos *foreground* this man, who has come to be known (in video adaptation titles and descriptions) as "the background walker." These adaptations all make fun of the stereotypical person in the background of news interviews, who seems to just want to get on television. Yet, the videos vary in terms of how ridiculous the actions of the background walker become and whether or not he/she speaks. Some seem to want to match his movements exactly. Others feature a background walker who does any number of things to call attention to him or herself, including walking faster, looking at the camera more often, dancing, speaking during the interview, and changing costumes between the walk-across moments.

RESPONSE VIDEOS AND CAMP: REVISITED

Like Dodson adapters, many Sweet Brown adapters used parody and camp to contest something about the original video, context, genre, or situation. BarrettTV, who made a response video as Antoine Dodson, created another video after Sweet Brown's news interview (as shown in figure 3.1). He begins by donning his Dodson costume and speaking to the camera. He is then interrupted by Sweet Brown, whom he also plays, in blackface. As Dodson, he states, "Maybe you didn't know, honey, but I am the only black person that's gonna make a fool outta myself on YouTube and get famous, okay?" The video becomes a competition between Dodson and Brown. Brown, who is "giving an interview right now" interrupts Dodson with, "I almost died in a fire! Lord Jesus, help me, oh yessa, yessa, massa, oh lord help me please."[23] Mary J. Blige, whom BarrettTV plays in whiteface, then interrupts both Dodson and Brown. Blige holds a microphone, wears a leather coat, and sings about what's in Burger King's new chicken wrap—a parody of a Burger King commercial that never aired (it was "pulled, due to racial discrepancies") but was leaked onto YouTube in April 2012.[24] The three continue to fight about which one deserves to be famous, talking and singing over each other, none backing down. The characters work together to perform a history of black celebrities and cewebrities who seem willing to perform racial stereotypes for money or fame.

Another woman tags her video "Sweet Brown," though Brown does not come up in the interview. Rather, the woman plays two characters: a news anchor, and Lemonjelly Jenkins (pronounced L'a*mon*gela). This video parodies the news genre, and people who give news interviews. Like Brown, Lemonjelly offers an excess of personal information in her interview. Lemonjelly stands in a Kmart vest on a lawn, as shown in figure 3.2, and speaks to the camera:

> I am so mad right now! I had to call off my job for this, cuz they want to burn down my apartment complex. I know who it was, too, I know who it was. It was Michael, it was Greg, it was Chris, and it was Marc. Cuz they mad at our landlord, cuz he don't be doin' stuff, and we called The Department of Health, and they was like 'Oh well we can't do nothing about it,' so they got . . . you know what? Our landlord gonna get his, he gonna get his.
> *(Lemonjelly yells to someone off camera)*

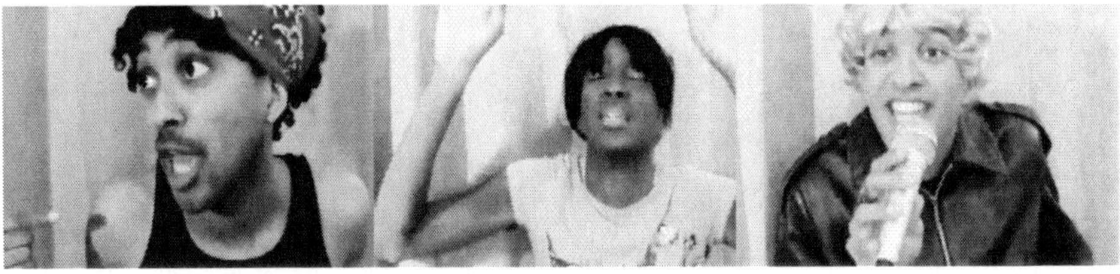

Figure 3.1. Screenshots of Antoine Dodson, Sweet Brown, and Mary J. Blige, as performed by BarrettTV in "Sweet Brown is on Fire! (Parody)."
***Source*: Screenshots courtesy of BarrettTV.**

No, I'm tellin' on them, girl, cuz I can't read your Facebook no more! So stupid! Dumb fools! Ooh, I'm so mad at them!
(Lemonjelly pauses, then speaks to the camera again.)
This on national TV, right? You know what, Rico? I got something for you, baby, I got something for you, sugar pie. Remember you said we gonna be together forever? We even got matching tattoos . . . Uh huh, you called me a fool last night, Rico. Don't nobody call me a fool, Rico . . . Yo, check this out, fool.
(Lemonjelly shows off her asymmetrical haircut, and the scar from her assumedly recently removed tattoo.)
Long hair, *psych*! Long hair, *psych*! In your face, Rico! Tellin' on the criminal, tellin' on the criminal![25]

Lemonjelly's eyewitness account becomes a personal tirade for the entire viewing audience, which she assumes includes Rico. The deadpan expression on the news anchor's face after the on-the-scene interview, as seen in figure 3.3, shows her disapproval of Lemonjelly's behavior on camera.

Creators like NikkieDe and BarrettTV use camp and parody to make statements about representations of black Americans on television, performing racial stereotypes as a springboard to fame, and/or using the television news as a platform for personal messages. A much younger boy, meanwhile, also plays both interviewer and Sweet Brown in his remake, to make a simpler, yet similar statement. As Sweet Brown, he wears a washcloth on his head, and alters his voice (to make it higher in pitch) using editing software. As the interviewer, he asks Sweet Brown, "How could burning wood smell like a barbecue? Are you stupid?" As

Figure 3.2. Screenshot, "In your face, Rico!" Lemonjelly Jenkins, as performed by NikkieDe.
***Source*: Screenshot courtesy of NikkieDe.**

Figure 3.3. Screenshot of expression on news anchor's face after Lemonjelly Jenkins's interview.
***Source*: Screenshot courtesy of NikkieDe.**

Sweet Brown, he responds, "I'm not stupid, fool! I'm on TV!"[26] The boy insults Sweet Brown's intelligence in this adaptation, insinuating that her answers to the news reporter's questions are inane, and that *she* believes the television appearance itself will make her appear smart regardless of what she says.

RACIAL REPRESENTATION ON TELEVISION NEWS

According to J. Fred MacDonald, "the African American lower class and urban underclass . . . have traditionally been relegated to the crime and mayhem stories reported on TV newscasts. And since such reportage rarely explains lower-class failures in terms of root causes, the emerging picture is one of lawlessness brought about by poor citizens all by themselves."[27] Sally Lehrman et al. similarly point out that the news media "has lost sight of the importance of fair and comprehensive reporting on issues related to race," resulting in "a huge gap between the perception of the state of minorities in America and their actual status."[28] According to Lehrman et al., "there are still two American experiences for people of color–the one they live and the one whites think they live" and "the [news] media have helped perpetuate misconceptions about the state of minorities in America," ultimately maintaining a cycle of structural racism in the news media.[29]

One vlogger (who acknowledges his videos are often laced with profanity[30]) expresses his frustration that the news media seem to look for a certain type of person for on-the-scene interviews. In reference to Sweet Brown's interview, he states:

> Why, YouTube, why? Why did they interview this bitch? Now I gotta unzip my blackness, and I just got it back. You wanna know what's so offensive about this video? I'll tell you. This mammy-looking bitch looks like she's about to start serving the news crew pancakes. Like, I swear this bitch was in the background of the movie *The Color Purple*. This is flamboyant coonery at its finest. . . . I still don't know why news crews go for these kinds of people when they look for interviews. How is this bitch's information at all relevant? "I got up to get a pop and then I smelt some barbeque!" I would much rather them show a burnt house for 10 minutes. That black dude in the background is pacing back and forth like, "Man, get this bitch off camera. I am offended right now!"[31]

That "black dude in the background" (i.e., the background walker), however, is Sweet Brown's son, Stanford. In an interview with Linda Cavanaugh on KFOR-TV, Stanford explains that he saw the camera crews setting up, and his mother "just came out of nowhere" hoping to be interviewed. Stanford then told Sweet Brown, "Look, Mom, do not say anything crazy." It seems, however, that she did. Stanford paced back and forth behind her during the interview, his hands to his face during one walk-across, and a glance at his mother during the second. Stanford said that only days later people were knocking on their door, wanting to take pictures with them, saying that the interview "made everybody's day."[32]

During the KFOR-TV interview, Sweet Brown tells Cavanaugh, "It's been really fun," because she's "never experienced anything like this before." Cavanaugh asks Brown, "Is that how you usually are? How did all of this stuff come up in your mind?" Stanford, not missing a beat, chimes in: "That's how she is." Sweet Brown responds, "It just came to my mind *like I was reading a script,* and I was reading my mind." Stanford confirms again, "That's her, that's her! She talks exactly like that." Brown ends the interview stating, "I'm glad to be here. I'm glad to make everyone's day. It's wonderful, and I'm glad to be Sweet Brown."[33]

The comment responses to the vlogger mentioned above insult his "blackness," masculinity, and assumed sexuality. YouTube user wootdogg2000 comments, "Why you talking hell u ain't black yo ass high yellow trying to take her fame! Lol get cha own." YouTube user Tamara Wagner states, "You are a black hipster douche. Ain't nobody got time for that!'" YouTube user Legally Arrested, meanwhile, states that natesvlog's video "is very racist" and that there is "no need for mean remarks especially when she has such a nice and peaceful personality just look at her interviews. She is very caring, and hasn't hurt anybody . . . AIN'T NOBODY GOT TIME FOR YOUR HATEFUL COMMENTS." InTolt991, further, comments, "This guy is an idiot! You don't sound educated at all.

Sweet Brown isn't hurting anyone, she looks like a nice woman. And she is a mother so when u call her a bitch u punk bitch . . . think of your mom being called a bitch!" It seems that many more people were insulted by this vlogger's insinuations than they were by the Sweet Brown interview.[34]

ALL IN THE FAMILY ROOM: CHILD REENACTORS AND RACIAL INNOCENCE

A large number of the Sweet Brown reenactments on YouTube star young children—children as young as one. Sweet Brown has infiltrated family rooms, living rooms, kitchens, and bedrooms in the United States and beyond. Home videos of children imitating Brown are proudly displayed on YouTube, some videos created by the children themselves, and some by the parents or other adult caregivers. Many of the older children perform Brown's interview word for word. The younger kids, however, have a more difficult time getting the words straight. A young girl in a red bandana (à la Dodson) imitates Sweet Brown, stating, "I said Oh Lord Jesus I have some fire." An older woman, meanwhile, interviews a 6-year-old girl, who performs as Sweet Brown. The girl explains, "I woke up to get me a freeze pop and I ran outside with no shoes on! It's too early! Barbecue! There's a fire! And the smoke got me! I had [unintelligible]. Ain't nobody got time for that."[35] The girl then begins singing the autotune remix. A two-year-old boy, filmed by his parents, yells enthusiastically, "I like cold pop! Oh Jesus, it's a farm! I didn't grab no shoes or anything, Jesus! I ran for my life! The smoke got me! I got vronchitis!"[36] The boy grabs his throat, and in one word, explains, "Ainnomoneygottimefodat!" One proud mother posted a video of her son in May 2012, impersonating "the classic Sweet Brown video."[37] Sweet Brown had become a classic, in the eyes of this parent, in only a month. A proud Canadian father, meanwhile, boasts in his video's description: "This is a parody of my son acting out the sweet brown monologue. I am very proud of him as he is only three years old. If you watch this please pass it along. I hope sweet brown can see this video I think she would be proud."[38] The boy is very animated, and remains quite faithful to Brown's interview text. The video is shot in four takes, assumedly by the father, from several angles.

Paratexts of these Sweet Brown adaptations indicate that many of the videos are made "just for fun." The video adaptations could also be looked at as cultural performances, which, as Victor Turner states, are "flexible and nuanced instruments capable of carrying and communicating many messages at once, even of subverting on one level what it appears to be 'saying' on another."[39] YouTube adaptations constitute a genre of cultural performance, performances that "are not simple mirrors but magical mirrors of social reality: they exaggerate, invert, re-form, magnify, minimize, dis-color, re-color, even deliberately falsify, chronicled events."[40] BarrettTV and NikkieDe, through their satirical, campy performances, echo older problematic scripts regarding representations of black Americans on television, reminding the audience of the past, and the present's relation to it. Meanwhile, the videos starring children perpetuate racial stereotypes guiltlessly through the "racial innocence" of child reenactors.

Robin Bernstein defines racial innocence as "a form of deflection, a not-knowing or obliviousness that can be made politically useful."[41] According to Bernstein, "When a racial argument is effectively countered or even delegitimized in adult culture, the argument often flows stealthily into children's culture or performances involving children's bodies. So located, the argument appears racially innocent. This appearance of innocence provides a cover under which otherwise discredited racial ideology survives and continues, covertly, to influence culture."[42] Additionally, "pop cultures of childhood have delivered, in fragmented and distorted forms, the images, practices, and ideologies of . . . minstrelsy well into the twentieth century." Bernstein explicitly connects childhood innocence to "the production of racial memory through the performance of forgetting." In the form of "forgotten surrogation," the lost original "doubles upon the construction of childhood itself as a process of loss and forgetting."[43] This theory could be applied to the Sweet Brown child reenactors on YouTube. The history of minstrel performances is likely unknown to the children who re-perform Sweet Brown's interview. The parents, meanwhile, ignore or overlook these problematic historical scripts, so they might focus on their child's cuteness, talent at memorizing, improvising, and/or performing. Stereotypes of black Americans and echoes of the minstrel tradition are thus maintained "accidentally."

Meanwhile, the child is often "getting it live," as Rebecca Schneider would say, in his/her reenactment. The child loses text, or context, and changes the performance through misquotes. Schneider sees these types of mistakes as inherently generative, stating, "Is error necessarily failure? When is difference failure, and by what (geohistorical, chronopolitical) standard?" Schneider points out that "if repetition is what we're condemned to do if we do not remember adequately, repetition is also . . . a mode of remembering—a remembering that, somehow, might place history's mistakes at hand, as if through repeated enactment we could avoid . . . repetition."[44] The recorded and digitally archived performances of these children preserve a sort of spirit of the minstrel performance, through their voices and bodies. Further, these online videos may or may not still be around for possible future generations to access, with even less context, yet still including the myriad "mistakes" the performing children have made.

REENACTMENT AND SCRIPTIVE THINGS

Video-to-video adaptations on YouTube, in general, can be compared to Robin Bernstein's concept of the "scriptive thing," which, like a play script, "broadly structures a performance while allowing for agency, and unleashing original, live variations that may not be individually predictable." Bernstein explains the scriptive thing as "interactive," as "the word 'script' captures the moment when dramatic narrative and movement through space are in the act of becoming each other." Bernstein further states that "when scriptive things enter a repository, repertoires arrive with them. Within a brick-and-mortar archive, scriptive things archive the repertoire—partially and richly, with a sense of openness and flux. To read things as scripts is to coax the archive into divulging the repertoire."[45] And though YouTube is not a "brick-and-mortar archive" it is most certainly an archive in which a variety of users make and re-make videos based on other videos they've seen in the archive.

Rebecca Schneider extends Bernstein's concept of the "scriptive thing" to the camera. The camera is "a scriptive thing shaping [a] woman's pose and ensuring that the pose will, itself, become a thing to stand beside, look at, hold in the archive . . . thus, recurring in the future it casts forward as a hail." Schneider asks:

> If the pose, or even the accident captured as snapshot, is a kind of hail cast into a future moment of its invited recognition, then can that gestic call in its stilled articulation be considered, somehow, live? Or, at least, re-live? Can we think of the still not as an artifact of non-returning time, but as situated in a live moment of its encounter that it, through its articulation as gesture or hail, predicts? This is to ask: is the stilled image a call toward a future live moment when the image will be re-encountered, perhaps as an invitation to response? And if so, *is it not live—taking place in time in the scene of its reception?*[46]

Cameras are scriptive things, and photographs re-live in the moment of encounter by an audience. It follows that this can also be extended to video—particularly online videos that are freely accessible to a large public, who may watch them at any time. These videos become not so much evidence of a time past, as real-time invitations to participate in the cycle of cultural production. The video camera, television news genre, and the YouTube video are scriptive things, feeding off each other to create a culture of event and subsequent creative, performative, poly-vocal response: video dialogue. Deitmar Offenhuber notes the importance of "social software" (like YouTube) in creating a dialogue, rather than a collection of individual pieces. Social software shifts our "attention from the individual piece to the creative ecosystem from which that piece evolves: a video that seems derivative appears more meaningful if understood as an element of an improvisational dialogue among many authors."[47]

Yet, cultural transmission via the family and home movies is muddied on the popular/public platform of YouTube. Each adult or child that re-performs Antoine Dodson or Sweet Brown and uploads a video of the performance onto YouTube is adding another file to the growing archive of documents that share, preserve, perpetuate, and question the transmission of culture through performance. Meanwhile, no matter what a re-performance does—refer, perform, question, command—it always evaluates, and thus always has an ethical dimension. Regardless of technical accuracy, each new face/voice in this re-performance carnival carries with it a unique tone, which carries with *it* an "imprint of individuality," the shadings of which are infinitely complex.[48] Tone evidences the act's singularity, for each video upload, and "the responsibility of the participants," performer and viewer alike.[49]

TOMITUDES, MINSTRELSY, AND MEMES

Adaptations of Antoine Dodson and Sweet Brown are similar, in several ways, to the "Tomitude." Tomitudes, stage adaptations of Harriett Beecher Stowe's novel *Uncle Tom's Cabin*, could be considered an early performance meme. Stowe's novel was released in serial form several years before copyright law was extended to dramatic productions of literary works. According to Eric Lott, "something of the immediacy of [the] impact [of *Uncle Tom's Cabin*] may be gauged from the fact that its first stage production occurred during its serialization, before the book appeared. Since no law existed copyrighting fictional material for stage use, adapters were free to appropriate at will."[50] Indeed, more people saw the story as a stage play or musical than read the book. Lott estimates that at least three million people saw these plays, ten times the book's first-year sales. Tomitudes were also "perfectly situated to infiltrate [the] cultural sphere in a way Stowe's novel had been unable to do. Their chief theatres, such as the National, the Bowery, the American Museum, and the Franklin Museum, were well known for their ability to cater to the million."[51] While two theatrical adaptations, created by George Aiken and H. J. Conway, were the most well-known, performance adaptations of *Uncle Tom's Cabin* quickly dominated popular culture in the northern United States, as "the theatrical world was crowded with offshoots, parodies, thefts, and rebuttals of every imaginable kind" for several years.[52] Anti-slavery, moderate, and pro-slavery versions of the play coexisted, and were all—to some extent—"informed by the devices of the minstrel show."[53] According to Lott, "to produce the play was by definition to engage in a divisive cultural struggle," and the political consequence of this struggle was "heated journalistic and street debate," despite producers' attempts to incorporate melodrama, to tone down the play.[54]

Henry James states, about his own experiences viewing both Aiken's and Conway's versions of the play:

> If the amount of life represented in such a work is measurable by the ease with which representation is taken up and carried further, carried even violently further, the fate of Mrs. Stowe's picture was conclusive; it simply sat down wherever it lighted and made itself, so to speak, at home; thither multitudes flocked afresh and there, in each case, it rose to its height again and went, with all its vivacity and good faith, through all its motions.[55]

James uses the metaphor of a "leaping fish" to describe how *Uncle Tom's Cabin* took over the culture industry. Uncle Tom "leaps from the page . . . with no apparent link to the mechanics of production ('printed, published, sold, bought and 'noticed') or of form."[56] Uncle Tom was simultaneously Stowe's work of fiction and somehow a living being, as James insinuates, "making itself, so to speak, at home." Uncle Tom was a "cultural force," politically potent, iconographic in popular culture, and "revolutionary in its effortless and near-immediate replication everywhere."[57] According to Lott, the story "so transcended the usual media of culture that it put an uncanny new spin on one's *relation* to the culture. Uncle Tom was at once all places and specifiably nowhere."[58]

There are several similarities between Tomitudes and the Dodson and Brown video adaptation trends. A variety of ideologies and styles were present in Tomitudes, as there are in the Dodson and Brown adaptations. YouTube also has the ability to cater to the multiple-millions, and "infiltrate the cultural sphere," and like YouTube, the stage adaptations of *Uncle Tom's Cabin* could reach many non-literate peoples. Recording and performing rights were not extended to nondramatic literary works until 1953.[59] While extending copyright law to encapsulate performance adaptations may have effectively squashed the everyday instinct to display creative adaptations publicly for many people after 1953, this instinct returns with YouTube video adaptations, and the current muddy copyright laws regarding many of these videos (like the "Hitler Reacts to" videos I discuss in chapter 4).

According to Taylor and Austen, "today, minstrelsy and 'tomming' are almost synonymous," but this was not true in the nineteenth century, when the Uncle Tom and the minstrel show certainly "intersected," but "were at heart quite different entertainments."[60] Regardless of ideology, for example, the majority of the Uncle Tom shows were intended for white audiences, while some minstrel shows were not. Additionally, blackface performance and minstrelsy are not synonymous. Due to what Taylor and Austen call "historical amnesia," along with general confusion, "'minstrelsy' has been redefined to mean any behavior that invokes demeaning black stereotypes for a white audience," regardless of whether or not these stereotypes were seen in actual minstrel shows, and regardless of who the audiences were for these shows (i.e., white or black audiences).[61] The authors go on to explain the discomfort many contemporary audiences experience with "classic" blackface, and how "pain, insult, and shock may overwhelm any instinct to chuckle, so [audiences] can't be faulted for not associating minstrelsy with comedy."[62] Additionally, the use of the term minstrelsy today "seems to draw on only certain aspects of the black minstrel tradition: lowbrow African American performances of stereotypes for an audience that includes whites."[63]

Dodson and Brown have both been accused of perpetuating minstrel stereotypes through their news interviews. It follows, then, that the adaptations of the Dodson and Brown videos would also perpetuate minstrel traditions—especially the reenactments and remakes that do little to overtly critique the interview(s). Regarding reenactments, Rebecca Schneider states that the first time a performance is done, it is "on target," while the second (or any subsequent) time "is way off, late, minor, drag, DIY, any-clown-can-do-it."[64] Schneider continues, positing that if the first time is "true," this makes the subsequent times "false, etiolated, hollow, or infelicitous . . . [and ultimately] lesser."[65] Meanwhile, this "lesser" performance "gain[s] a kind of agency in the re-do . . . [as] the idea that 'anyone can do it' takes the nascent shape of hope . . . troubling the prerogatives of linear time."[66] By creating a re-performance of Antoine Dodson or Sweet Brown, creators have some agency in the re-do. They are thus bringing up not only questions about the returns of the history of the original news interviews, but also questions about black performances in popular culture, and how these performances are received and interpreted.

Eric Lott states that as "one of our earliest culture industries, minstrelsy not only affords a look at the emergent historical break between high and low cultures, but also reveals popular culture to be a place where cultures of the dispossessed are routinely commodified—and contested."[67] While some of the Dodson and Brown adaptation videos mirror minstrelsy in image and style, the videos do not necessarily reflect the ideological intent(s) of blackface minstrelsy, or even knowledge of this history. Rather, these adaptations similarly show YouTube as a popular sphere where current "cultures of the dispossessed" are being both commodified and contested. According to Lott, "at every turn blackface minstrelsy has seemed a form in which transgression and containment coexisted, in which improbably threateningly or startlingly sympathetic racial meanings were simultaneously produced and dissolved."[68] The variety of Dodson and Brown video adaptations, if looked at through the lens of minstrelsy, also offer possibilities for simultaneous transgression and containment.

Additionally, according to Taylor and Austen, despite how one might feel about white performers doing minstrel shows in blackface, black minstrels were sometimes operating on a different level altogether. As black performers "transmogrified white imitations of blackness, they brought in their own cultural traditions, and they used the forum and form to practice entertainment innovations that still powerfully resonate."[69] The authors explain that, since emancipation, "black performers have alternately embraced, exploited, subverted, and turned stereotypes inside out, quite often becoming tremendously successful with both black and white audiences in the process."[70] While many critics have suggested that these black performers were "forced to indulge in demeaning caricatures or wear blackface, . . . in fact, [many] knew exactly what they were doing: they often had alternatives, and had good reasons for choosing to draw from the minstrel tradition."[71] Using Burt Williams as their main example, Taylor and Austen argue that Williams "enjoyed himself and the minstrel tradition he partook in, and surely does not need our pity. For by pitying Bert Williams, we rob him of agency, deny the fact that he had options, and fail to respect his choices."[72] Taylor and Austen additionally point out that throughout US history, "[W]hites have had the freedom to choose any ['negative'] traits without being accused of anything worse than playing to the crowd. But whenever a black performer chooses a persona featuring ['negative'] traits . . . the accusation of minstrelsy tends to follow."[73]

On one hand, by calling Sweet Brown a "mammy" type, or pitying her, we forget that she was doing a news interview of her own volition, and not putting on a minstrel show. Brown also seems to have no regrets about her interview, and even has a sense of humor about being a YouTube sensation. Her "web redemption" on *Tosh.0* shows this (discussed below, particularly the cut footage), along with other interviews she has given. On the other hand, is it possible that Brown perhaps exhibits the "double-consciousness" of black Americans that W.E.B. Du Bois writes about; the "sense of always looking at one's self through the eyes of others, of measuring one's soul by the tape of a world that looks on in amused contempt and pity?"[74] Is it possible or worthwhile to try to determine how Sweet Brown's news performance may have been intentionally or unintentionally crafted for this specific audience: the "world that looks on in amused contempt and pity"? Or can we just let Sweet Brown say she was being herself, and that she's happy, and leave it at that?

According to Taylor and Austen:

> Raucous comedy, clownish demeanor, rural cuisine, exaggerated expressions, and 'dirty laundry' can all be drawn from both real-life experience and theatrical traditions developed in the days of burnt cork. But codes of dignity and masculinity, inner struggles caused by Du Boisian 'double consciousness,' and spoken and unspoken mandates to uplift the race have pressured generations of black artists to keep these themes and inspirations in check.[75]

While Sweet Brown may not be an artist, and may have been less self-consciously performing herself for the news interview, the many Sweet Brown adapters are creating a cultural product that is more akin to an art object and thus must answer to this double consciousness. Taylor and Austen also point out that since the beginning of black minstrelsy, "African American artists have demonstrated that masking and foolishness can provide freedom as well as bondage."[76] Are Dodson and Brown re-performances using the "masks" of Antoine Dodson and Sweet Brown to be free to perform passionately? Or are these re-performances shackled by how people receive any performance that deals in humor and race or class stereotyping? Bert William's personal theory about comedy was that "troubles are only funny when you pin them to one particular individual."[77] Following this theory, by giving faces to the specific problems in the Dodson and Brown news interviews, the news stations opened the stories up to humorous interpretations. But because these humorous interpretations are loaded with the baggage of racial and class stereotyping they are controversial, and no one seems to know who to blame or how to handle the controversy.

CEWEBRITY AND AUTHENTICITY

Brown's sense of humor about being a "YouTube Sensation," makes her seem authentic, likeable, and sympathetic. On this note, Sweet Brown was invited to appear on *Tosh.0,* a television show on Comedy Central starring comedian Daniel Tosh. According to the *Tosh.0* website, "[Daniel] Tosh has established himself as the preeminent expert on exhibitionist weirdos, injurious idiots and the best worst things on the Web."[78] As Hank Stuever of *The Washington Post* states, while sometimes funny, the show's cruelty is "as black as the online soul, and as fleeting and ephemeral," which results in a "blundering exploration of race, class, gender, [and] life."[79] One of the show's hallmarks is the "web redemption," which Tosh offers to people who are perceived as doing or saying embarrassing things in viral internet videos. Yet the nature of these so-called redemptions is often a further exploitation or embarrassment of the person or people who are already facing public shame from their viral internet videos.

Sweet Brown accepted the show's invitation, and her web redemption was televised on October 9, 2012. While the entire interview was not televised, cut footage was available for viewing on Tosh's website. The cut footage sheds some light on how Brown's redemption was framed for the aired version of the show. Many sections of the interview that humanize Sweet Brown and make her appear more worldly and intelligent, like Tosh and Brown joking and laughing with each other about politics, weather, and family, were cut for the aired version. One bit of humor between Daniel Tosh and Sweet Brown that did make the cut involves her father, as Sweet Brown states that as she ran out of her apartment during the fire, she forgot her Daddy who was "in the closet." When Tosh responds, "Why is your Daddy in the closet? In this day and age, it's time to come out," Sweet Brown laughs heartily and explains: "He's cremated. . . . And I left him in the closet!"[80]

Meanwhile, the aired web redemption footage ends with "Sweet Brown's Urban Fire Safety Tips," a Public Service Announcement that Brown agrees to make for the urban population. At this point, any morale the web redemption might have had is lost. Brown's superhero persona—she is wearing a shiny superwoman-style costume, which she laughingly questions in the interview's cut footage—capitalizes on a number of poor, urban stereotypes, and lacks any real sense of redemption. For example, Brown warns some kids playing in water spraying from a fire hydrant, "This water's for fire spraying, not sidewalk playing! That's wasteful! Ain't nobody got time for that!" Brown smiles at the camera and her gold tooth gleams, unnaturally (a special effect added by the show). Brown then dumps a bucket of water on two homeless men heating their hands over a grill, stating "This is a public space, not your fireplace! That's dangerous! Ain't nobody got time for that!" She smiles at the camera again, and her gold tooth gleams. Following this, Brown dumps a bucket of water on a man who is smoking crack, and states "If you smoke the rock, you'll burn down the whole block! Ain't nobody got time for that!" She smiles at the camera, and her gold tooth gleams. The PSA ends as Sweet Brown dumps a bucket of water on Daniel Tosh and his friend, who are playing a basketball videogame. As she dumps the water, Brown exclaims, "Boom shaka-laka! . . . When you score three baskets in a row, you hot enough to melt the flo'! Ain't nobody got time for that!"[81] This time, however, she does not smile. Her gold tooth flashes anyway, as she closes her mouth after speaking. The look on her face is puzzling, and that final awkward tooth glimmer leaves me feeling that the interview was more exploitative than redemptive, after all, as Tosh's web redemptions often are.

While Brown was surprised and unassuming after her news interview went viral, Dodson capitalized on his cewebrity status openly and vigorously. This makes him seem more like a character, and less likeable as a *real* person. Dodson, arguably, willingly became a caricature of how he was presented in the news interview in his many future public television appearances.[82]

In doing so, Dodson put a price tag on his family's tragedy. Live musical performances reveal he's an awful singer, even when autotuned; this adds another dent into his authenticity. Antoine Dodson seems to be performing "Dodson" in many contexts, while Sweet Brown just seems like she is "being herself" all over the place. With Dodson, anti-theatrical prejudice seems to combine with the anti-capitalist sentiments of online sharing economies like YouTube. This, along with no news in terms of finding the accused rapist, turns Dodson into a sort of YouTube pariah.

Is it perhaps easier or funnier to parody a pariah? Or is it more excusable to laugh at? Whereas Brown adaptations go out of their way to claim "just for fun" status, Dodson adaptations do not. Rather, Dodson video adaptations' titles and paratexts often explain that the videos are meant to be "hilarious," "funny," and "ridiculous," like the original Dodson interview video. In doing so, the adapters appear to be making fun of Dodson, rather than just having fun like many Sweet Brown adapters. Meanwhile, the potential instinct for video-makers to contest the overall Dodson situation through video adaptation is overshadowed by how Dodson has continued to play "Dodson" for financial gain, with ambiguous moral and ethical limits and goals. While Brown does appear in a few commercials, advertising for property realtors and dentists, for example, the overall half-life of her video meme was shorter and a bit quieter than Dodson's. Somehow, all of this considered together seems to make Brown more "authentic" as a person, and not just another money-and-fame-hungry cewebrity like Dodson.

NOTES

1. The Parody Factory, "Sweet Brown—Ain't Nobody Got Time for That (Autotune Remix)," YouTube, Apr. 13, 2012, accessed Sept. 21, 2012, https://www.youtube.com/watch?v=bFEoMO0pc7k.
2. Popularity determined by number of views by Sept. 21, 2013. The video has over 58 million views on YouTube as of Sept. 2016.
3. Dietmar Offenhuber, *Transformative Copy*, MS Thesis, Media Arts and Sciences (School of Architecture and Planning, Massachusetts Institute of Technology, Feb. 2008), 37.
4. deznell, "SWEET BROWN QUARTET," YouTube, Apr. 22, 2012, accessed Sept. 21, 2012, https://www.youtube.com/watch?v=Mfav0yvcaks.
5. Rodney Oliver Banks, "SWEET BROWN COLD POP INSPIRATIONAL REMIX by Rodney Oliver Banks," YouTube, May 24, 2012, accessed Sept. 21, 2012. (Video has been removed from YouTube.)
6. Banks, "SWEET BROWN COLD POP."
7. poeticstarlet94, "Sweet Brown COGIC Remix," YouTube, Apr. 25, 2012, accessed Sept. 21, 2012. (Video has been removed from YouTube.)
8. StatusMusicDesign, "Ain't Nobody Got Time For That (Less Than 1 min. Acoustic . . . Parody?)," YouTube, June 25, 2012, accessed Sept. 20, 2013, https://www.youtube.com/watch?v=wMVCOPgKPz4.
9. James M. Dorman, "Shaping the Popular Image of Post-Reconstruction American Blacks: The 'Coon Song' Phenomenon of the Gilded Age," *American Quarterly* 40 (1988), 455.
10. Richard A. Reublin and Robert L. Maine, "Question of the Month: What Were Coon Songs?" Jim Crow Museum of Racist Memorabilia Website, Ferris State University, May 2005, accessed Oct. 1, 2013, http://www.ferris.edu/HTMLS/news/jimcrow/question/may05/index.htm.
11. Yuval Taylor and Jake Austen, *Darkest America: Black Minstrelsy from Slavery to Hip-Hop* (New York: Norton, 2012), Kindle edition, loc. 2895–900.
12. Taylor and Austen, *Darkest America*, loc. 4047.

13. Taylor and Austen, *Darkest America,* loc. 1888.
14. Taylor and Austen, *Darkest America,* loc. 2657.
15. Greg Spencer, "Pepsi Next Commercial: Sweet Brown Parody," YouTube, May 10, 2012, accessed Aug. 20, 2012, https://www.youtube.com/watch?v=OXgGs6qqOQg.
16. Lauryn Joleigh, "Cocoa Brown (Sweet Brown Parody)," YouTube, July 29, 2012, accessed Aug. 20, 2012, https://www.youtube.com/watch?v=xfrbX0dsELU.
17. Paige Yarbrough, "Sweet Brown Remake," YouTube, July 31, 2012, accessed Nov. 11, 2012, https://www.youtube.com/watch?v=WJnx2_kgb-Q.
18. youstillamazeme, "Sweet Brown ('Ain't Nobody Got Time for That' Remix)," YouTube, Apr. 12, 2012, accessed Sept. 21, 2012. (Video has been removed from YouTube.)
19. Valerie Toledo, "Sweet Brown Remix (Ain't Nobody Got Time for That) Music Video by the Arnaiz Crew," YouTube, Aug. 26, 2012, accessed Sept. 21, 2012, https://www.youtube.com/watch?v=vFUrbgGLa6s.
20. MessyMyles, "Sweet Brown's Cold Pop Escape (Spoof)," YouTube, Apr. 12, 2012, accessed Aug. 20, 2012, https://www.youtube.com/watch?v=GMRD6kqEB8E.
21. ReviewManify, "Sweet Brown: No Time for Bronchitis Cold Pop Escape (Parody)," YouTube, Apr. 12, 2012, accessed Aug. 20, 2012. (Video has been removed from YouTube.)
22. Kevin Scott, "Sparkle Johnson: No Time For Gay/Sweet Brown No Time for Bronchitis," YouTube, Apr. 20, 2012, accessed Aug. 20, 2012, https://www.youtube.com/watch?v=5fnuKPBrpSk.
23. BarrettTV, "Sweet Brown is on Fire! (Parody)," YouTube, Apr. 11, 2012, accessed Jan. 14, 2013, https://www.youtube.com/watch?v=tIqs1LbJWgM.
24. SophiaPetrillosBuddy, "Mary J. Blige Burger King Commercial," YouTube, April 4, 2012, accessed Jan. 14, 2013, https://www.youtube.com/watch?v=XukHU8y5GRQ.
25. NikkieDe, "Nicole got JOKES: L. Jenkins (News Parody) PART 2," YouTube, Apr. 13, 2012, accessed Sept. 19, 2013, https://www.youtube.com/watch?v=_fqyuflV93g.
26. SmartBoiiable, "No Time for Bronchitis (spoof)," YouTube, June 26, 2012, accessed Aug. 21, 2012, https://www.youtube.com/watch?v=lBAVLurDVeY.
27. J. Fred MacDonald, *Blacks and White TV: African Americans in Television Since 1948*, 2nd ed. (Chicago: Nelson-Hall, 1992), 279.
28. Sally Lehrman et al., *Evaluating Media Coverage of Structural Racism, Report* (Frisby & Associates, 2008), 122.
29. Lehrman et al., *Evaluating Media Coverage,* 122.
30. See Natesflicks, "YouTube's Bullshit Policies (What Happened to NatesVlogs?)," YouTube, Aug 16, 2014, accessed May 22, 2017, https://www.youtube.com/watch?v=4XvqLqTphAc.
31. YouTube user's name removed for anonymity, "Employee Evaluation: Sweet Brown Shames Black People," YouTube, Apr. 13, 2012, accessed Nov. 20, 2012. (Video has been removed from YouTube.)
32. Linda Cavanaugh, "Sweet Brown Sits Down with Us in Studio," KFOR-TV, April 16, 2012, accessed Jan. 14, 2013, http://kfor.com/2012/04/16/sweet-brown-sits-down-with-us-in-studio/.
33. Cavanaugh, "Sweet Brown Sits Down with Us."
34. These comments were written publicly in response to the vlog, "Employee Evaluation: Sweet Brown Shames Black People," YouTube, Apr. 13, 2012, accessed Nov. 20, 2012. (Video has been removed from YouTube.)
35. heidibell1979, "Sweet Brown Remake by 6yr Old," YouTube, Nov. 7, 2012, accessed Nov. 16, 2012, https://www.youtube.com/watch?v=xCc1KIvnngQ.
36. Kevin Michielsen, "Sweet Eli Brown," YouTube, July 30, 2012, accessed Nov. 16, 2012, https://www.youtube.com/watch?v=uxIaRnVIlJo.
37. Brent Brown, "5-year-old impersonates Sweet Brown," YouTube, May 13, 2012, accessed Nov. 16, 2012, https://www.youtube.com/watch?v=_4AxzpYpcn8.

38. B. Nelson, "Sweet Brown: No Time for Bronchitis (Toddler Parody)," YouTube, Nov. 5, 2012, accessed Nov. 16, 2012. (Video has been removed from YouTube.)

39. Victor Turner, *The Anthropology of Performance* (New York: PAJ Publications, 1988), 24.

40. Turner, *The Anthropology of Performance*, 42.

41. Robin Bernstein, *Racial Innocence: Performing American Childhood from Slavery to Civil Rights* (New York: New York University Press, 2011), Kindle edition, loc. 901.

42. Bernstein, *Racial Innocence*, loc. 1109.

43. Bernstein, *Racial Innocence*, loc. 574.

44. Rebecca Schneider, *Performing Remains: Art and War in Times of Theatrical Reenactment* (New York: Routledge, 2011), Kindle edition, 40.

45. Bernstein, *Racial Innocence*, loc. 13.

46. Schneider, *Performing Remains*, 141. (Emphasis added.)

47. Offenhuber, *Transformative Copy*, 32.

48. Gary Saul Morson and Caryl Emerson, *Mikhail Bakhtin: Creation of a Prosaics* (Stanford: Stanford University Press, 1990), 134.

49. Morson and Emerson, *Mikhail Bakhtin*, 134.

50. Eric Lott, *Love and Theft: Blackface Minstrelsy and the American Working Class* (New York: Oxford, 1993), 213.

51. Lott, *Love and Theft*, 227.

52. Lott, *Love and Theft*, 215.

53. Lott, *Love and Theft*, 212.

54. Lott, *Love and Theft*, 212.

55. Henry James, as quoted in Lott, *Love and Theft*, 215.

56. James as quoted in Lott, *Love and Theft*, 216.

57. Lott, *Love and Theft*, 216

58. Lott, *Love and Theft*, 216. (Emphasis in original.)

59. "Relevant Dates in US Copyright," *Express Permissions*, accessed Sept. 19, 2013, http://www.expresspermissions.com/rel_date.html.

60. Taylor and Austen, *Darkest America*, loc. 814–30.

61. Taylor and Austen, *Darkest America*, loc. 3172.

62. Taylor and Austen, *Darkest America*, loc. 3172.

63. Taylor and Austen, *Darkest America*, loc. 3140.

64. Schneider, *Performing Remains*, 180.

65. Schneider, *Performing Remains*, 180.

66. Schneider, *Performing Remains*, 180.

67. Lott, *Love and Theft*, 8.

68. Lott, *Love and Theft*, 234.

69. Taylor and Austen, *Darkest America*, loc. 4039.

70. Taylor and Austen, *Darkest America*, loc. 4039.

71. Taylor and Austen, *Darkest America*, loc. 151–59.

72. Taylor and Austen, *Darkest America*, loc. 1754–56.

73. Taylor and Austen, *Darkest America*, loc. 282.

74. W.E.B. Du Bois as quoted in Taylor and Austen, *Darkest America*, loc. 293.

75. Taylor and Austen, *Darkest America*, loc. 3374

76. Taylor and Austen, *Darkest America*, loc. 4047.

77. Bert Williams as quoted in Taylor and Austen, *Darkest America*, loc. 1525.

78. *Tosh.0*, "Home," Comedy Partners, 2016, accessed April 9, 2017, http://www.cc.com/shows/tosh.

79. Hank Steuver, "Comedy Central's 'Tosh.0': Five Years Later, It Hurts So Good," *The Washington Post*, Feb. 15, 2014, accessed May 3, 2015.

80. Daniel Tosh, "Web Redemption–Sweet Brown," Tosh.0, Comedy Central, accessed Jan. 14, 2013, http://tosh.comedycentral.com/video-clips/web-redemption---sweet-brown.

81. Tosh, "Web Redemption."

82. Including televised spots on "Tosh.0," "Lopez Tonight," and a Halloween costume contest on YouTube.

FOUR

Hitler . . . Played by Der Untergangers

We're crowded together in a bunker. The enemies are closing in on us, again. We steal furtive glances at each other from across the room and wait, as the always disheveled, sweaty, and delirious leader slowly takes off his eyeglasses, again. He speaks calmly, "Anyone with a blog or twitter account, leave the room now." Only three of us are left in the room after the mass file-out. There is another moment of tense silence, and then the leader breaks down. He has lost his mind once and for all, all over again. He screams, "What is wrong with these losers! This joke stopped being funny in 2008! I mean, Jesus Christ! This was only halfway clever the first time around! Now it's just a bunch of geek losers with iMovie jumping onto the latest nerd bandwagon! Don't these guys have lives!? Or jobs!? Or fucking girlfriends!? But no! They have to waste their time on some stupid internet in-joke!"

"I feel it is a clever subversion of traditional media," one of us says, hopefully. The leader doesn't miss a beat. His temper tantrum continues, again.

"Take your liberal arts bullshit and go back to Wesleyan! You know what would subvert MY idea of the internet? Some fucking originality! Instead of using the same old tired-ass joke to complain about how they changed the ending of the goddamn *Watchmen*! . . . Finally there is a mass medium open to everyone, and what do these pinheads do? Try to pass off this exercise in creative masturbation as something more than *pointless derivative bullshit*! And I don't care if they manage to sync the dialogue up *with Stalin*! I thought my legacy was secure. I slaughtered millions. Cut a bloody path of destruction across Europe. And for what? So I could be the latest juvenile web fad? No better than YouTube Fred or that stupid fucking hamster? And they don't even edit the clip! So I'm stuck endlessly complaining and complaining like some whiny-ass bitch!"

The leader sits, shakily, and takes a long, deep breath. He goes on, quietly, "I had such high hopes for original web content. I was even a beta tester for Strike TV. But this. This asinine *Downfall* fad. This confirms every stereotype about the internet, as just one self-referential circle-jerk among poorly socialized losers. What a goddamn waste!"[1]

His explosion does not surprise us. Hitler *always* reacts like this. He reacted in exactly the same way when he found out that his gaming account was banned from XBOX Live. And when he found out that he had to go see *Don't Mess with Zohan* because tickets for all the other movie screenings were sold out. And when he found out that Twitter was down for a day. And when he found out that Barack Obama would be visiting Berlin. And when he found out that *Harry Potter and the Deathly Hallows* was the last book in the series. And when he heard about the sub-prime mortgage crisis in the United States. And when he found out that his friends weren't going to Burning Man this year. And when Usain Bolt broke the 100-meter dash world record. And when Kanye West interrupted Taylor Swift's acceptance speech at the 2009 MTV Video Music Awards. And when Sarah Palin resigned from office. And when he found out everyone in his bunker was playing Pokémon Go. And when folks started comparing him to Donald Trump during the 2016 US presidential election season. And when, as hard as he tried, *he just could not find Waldo*. Hitler reacted exactly the same way, *almost* exactly the same way, to every last one of these events. Hitler has become quite a predictable fellow on YouTube these days.

This is, in part, thanks to Oliver Hirschbiegel's movie *Der Untergang* (English title: *Downfall*) (2004), which depicts Hitler's final days at the end of World War II.[2] The videos described above are all part of the popular *Downfall* internet video meme, also known as "Hitler reacts to" or "Hitler finds out" videos. The *Downfall* videos feature one scene in which Hitler, played by Bruno Ganz, throws a temper tantrum of epic proportions when he is informed that Germany has lost the war. This four-minute scene has inspired hundreds of thousands of video adaptations.[3] Video-makers use the original *Downfall* clip and the original actors' voices, but add new subtitles (in any language but German) so that Hitler seems to be reacting to some issue in popular culture, politics, sports, or everyday life. The above dialogue, for example, is from "Hitler Is Fed Up with All the Hitler Rants."[4] Similarly, in figure 4.1, Hitler is shown reacting to the "Hitler Reacts to" videos.

YouTube user DReaperF4 uploaded the first known *Downfall* parody to YouTube on August 10, 2006. The video was titled "Sim Heil: Der untersim" and subtitled in Spanish. It showed Hitler ranting about the lack of new features in the demo trial of Microsoft's videogame "Flight Simulator X." On August 30th, DReaperF4 uploaded an English version of "Sim Heil," making the joke accessible to English speaking players of the game. Since 2006, adaptations of the *Downfall* meme that use similar *creative subtitling* have multiplied exponentially. New videos appear on a daily basis, into 2016. These videos have even spawned a dedicated community of over 2,500 *Downfall* video creators who call themselves "Untergangers," roughly translated to English as "Downfallers." The Untergangers have made many *Downfall* videos, which they post daily to the group's website and to YouTube. They are dedicated to the archiving, creative continuation, and general evolution of the *Downfall* meme. The Untergangers are also an online community that offers creative support, feedback, chatting, gaming, and social networking opportunities for its members, in terms of their common interest in *Downfall* videos and other topics and areas of life not necessarily related to *Downfall.*[5]

In this chapter, I discuss the *Downfall* video meme as performances of adaptation. Focusing on the process of creative subtitling, I show how adapters use the movie *Downfall,* along with other *Downfall* parodies, as models for further creative acts, personal expression, and cultural commentary. Additionally, I offer the *Downfall* meme as one example of how everyday parodists and adapters have collectively been successful in terms of rebelling against and creatively navigating archaic copyright laws. While Siobhan O'Flynn suggests that "adaptation is (still) positioned consistently as a lesser, more simplistic mode of reworking content,"[6] the *Downfall* video meme exemplifies how these types of performances of adaptation can be socially complex ways of reworking *context.* Additionally, according to O'Flynn, "the affordances of the web and social networking platforms for viewing, remixing, sharing, and interacting with content include . . . numerous successful examples, if one bases success on popularity, longevity, and reach of dissemination."[7] The *Downfall* video adaptation trend is a relatively longstanding (i.e., "successful") example of how internet video memes can pique public interest in terms of both watching and creating video adaptations.

CULTURAL COMMENTARY VIA HITLER

This long-standing video meme shows how performance can be enacted through an Other (i.e., Hitler, or rather, a pre-existing performance of Hitler) to teach video-making skills to others, and as a safer and often humorous way to express personal opinions on sometimes touchy matters. The subtitler can perform through their unique subtitles, added to the video, without having to perform in the video corporeally or reveal his/her identity publicly. This "anonymous" performance works on two levels. First, it gives the person/group behind the subtitles the iconic status of speaking as Hitler. Anonymous personal and trivial problems or opinions seem far more important or interesting when they are performed to the tune of Bruno Ganz's expressive, emotional Hitler.

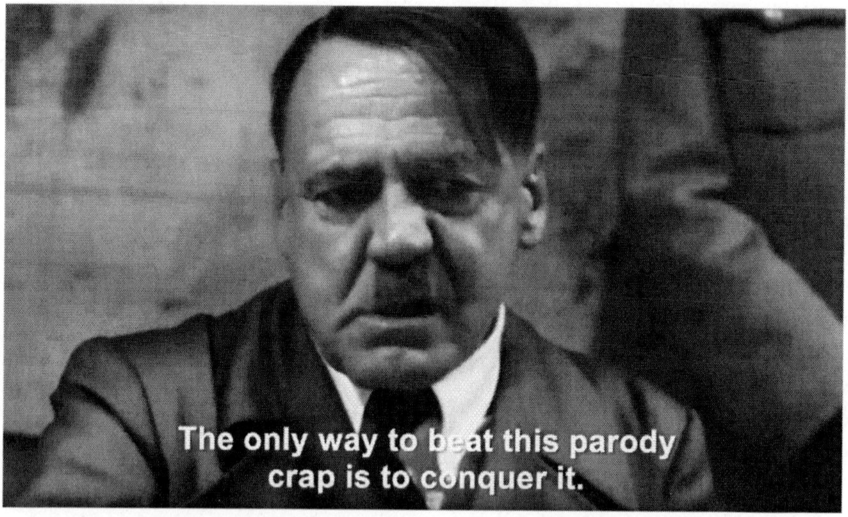

The only way to beat this parody
crap is to conquer it.

Figure 4.1. Screenshot of "Hitler Plans to Make a Downfall Parody."
***Source*: Screenshot courtesy of Hitler Rants Parodies.**

In "Hitler Gets Rick Rolled," for example, this everyday annoyance is stretched to grand proportions. Rickrolling is a sort of bait-and-switch Internet video meme that uses the music video from Rick Astley's song "Never Gonna Give You Up" (1987). The bait-and-switch involves sending a hyperlink where the web address reads as if it would logically lead to one type of source, but actually leads to Astley's video. Unsuspecting people who click on the link and are led to the music video have been *rickrolled*. In the video "Hitler Gets Rickrolled," his officers state that they have picked up some radio waves. When Hitler asks to listen to the radio waves, Astley's song begins to play. Hitler then spends the next three minutes furiously ranting about how this song and music video are destroying his quality of life, his ability to "have a quick wank," and his faith in internet links. Ultimately he concedes, "The power of that song is just unbelievable."[8]

In terms of why the "Hitler reacts to" meme is so popular, Virginia Heffernan of the *New York Times* speculates:

> We may have repressed that speak-for-the-people Hitler, the one he decided to be in "Mein Kampf"; but in the form of these videos, he has returned. Isn't that the outcome that Adolf Hitler, the historical figure, sought? Didn't he see himself as the brute voice of the everyman unconscious? How grim—how perplexing, how unsettling—that after more than 60 years of trying to cast and recast Hitler to make sense of him, we may have arrived at a version of Hitler that takes him exactly at his word.[9]

At the same time, putting these trivial, everyday matters into Hitler's mouth brings Hitler down to a sort of *anyman* status. I say anyman, rather than *everyman* (like Heffernan), because of the "I can see myself in his place" connotation of everyman. Few people would readily claim that they could relate to Hitler. And, while his responses in these videos generally do not include historically accurate information or even references to Nazi Germany, the character in the video can never be anyone besides Hitler. Rather, here, Hitler becomes an anyman—he still might be someone a viewer could relate to, yet he's still an *other*, some *other* person who has normal, stupid problems, just like anyone else. His specific problem, from video to video, is not universal. Instead, it is his overly emotional reaction to being out of the loop in some way, or to making a non-retractable mistake, that the viewer is asked to relate to or make fun of. In the subtitled scenes, Hitler is often some combination of weak, dumb, misinformed, and unreasonable. He is not up-to-date on current information—an inevitable phenomenon even for the many who have the means to access news online. Hitler's solutions to his various problems will also never work. Fans familiar with the *Downfall* meme know this even before watching the adaptations. His solutions can't work, because in "real" history, Germany lost the war, and that is what this scene is *really* about. Meanwhile, if there are any voices of reason present in the adaptation, Hitler ignores them. Overall, with these adaptations, it seems that if video makers and viewers are not necessarily ready or willing to identify or empathize with Hitler, they are at least open to knowing him—on their own terms. Thus, rather than saying, "I am just like that guy," the viewer can say, "I know someone just like that guy." "That guy" just so happens to be Bruno Ganz performing as Hitler. Potentially, any person who has ever longed to throw a childlike temper tantrum might relate to this Hitler. This Hitler belongs to a vast public, who are allowing themselves to put words in his mouth, laugh at his expense, and still—on some level—remember that this is a fictional portrayal of Hitler, performed by Bruno Ganz.

The persistence of this single meme also makes larger cultural statements. First, and foremost, Hitler can be funny. This is not necessarily a new idea (e.g., *The Great Dictator, The Producers*). These movies, however, were the products of major film corporations and well-known, popular auteur directors (Charlie Chaplin and Mel Brooks, respectively). The *Downfall* adaptation trend is the largest instance of a humorous Hitler that, while using footage from a major motion picture, speaks with the polyphonic, vernacular voice(s) of many people. Further, the tenacity of this video meme marks this type of subtitling as a skillful art and a legitimate means of creative expression.

When asked what he thought about such a serious scene being used for laughs, director Oliver Hirschbiegel responded that he believes the *Downfall* meme fits with the theme of the movie. According to Hirschbiegel, "[T]he point of the film was to kick these terrible people off the throne that made them demons, making them real and their actions into reality . . . I think it's only fair if now [the film is] taken as part of our history, and used for whatever purposes people like."[10] Hirschbiegel is even amused by many of the parodies, stating, "Someone sends me the links every time there's a new one. . . . Of course, I have to put the sound down when I watch. Many times the lines are so funny, I laugh out loud, and I'm laughing about the scene that I staged myself! You couldn't get a better compliment as a director."[11] A viewer who is offended by the use of Hitler as a comedic character under any circumstances is one thing. However, a viewer who finds the *Downfall* video meme (or a single *Downfall* adaptation) offensive may just not get the (inside) joke, which lies not in the literal translation of words but in the creative subtitling. On the other hand, a video creator who relies too much on accurate historical information about Nazi Germany in his or her video also does not understand the genre. The humor lies in the parody, juxtaposition, absurdity, and present-day relevance. It's not that the history of Nazi Germany is irrelevant, but rather that Bruno Ganz's portrayal of Hitler in Nazi Germany is being used by many others to express extreme, perhaps unreasonable, yet still relatable emotions.

A cartoon remake of Sweet Brown or an autotuned remix of Antoine Dodson (whom I discuss in chapters 2 and 3) will ultimately, always lead back to Brown and Dodson, who are real, living, people, capable of change and growth. The *Downfall* adaptations, though they star Ganz, will always lead back to Hitler. And Hitler will always be Hitler. All images that resemble Hitler become, to some degree, Hitler. As a social actor, his actions were far-reaching, destructive, and reprehensible, to say the very least. When attempting to write about Hitler (rather than Bruno Ganz performing Hitler), words begin to escape me. Hitler, at least for me, is often beyond language. We might still catch a glimpse here and there of Antoine Dodson and Sweet Brown remixes, or even Dodson and Brown themselves, online, as they were each briefly internet celebrities. Yet, Dodson's and Brown's celebrity has faded significantly in just a few years. Hitler's likely never will. Hitler's image has been used and re-used, cycled and recycled through many cultures for various purposes. As Heffernan states, we have been trying to "cast and recast" Hitler now for 60 years.[12] The casting of Bruno Ganz may have been the first step toward this "version" of Hitler we now have with the *Downfall* adaptations, but perhaps the movie was just a coincidence. Maybe it came out at just the right time, as internet and video technology were becoming more ubiquitous, just one year before the advent of YouTube.

Meanwhile, this version of Hitler we now have with the *Downfall* adaptations is also inextricable from Ganz's performance. Creatively subtitling other movies about Hitler, or creatively subtitling Hitler, would not fit within the meme. What *Downfall* offered that all the other versions and images and videos of Hitler (including Hitler the historical figure) do not offer was the perfect timing of its release, giving internet video makers a new performance of Hitler that had yet to be culturally cycled and recycled. It was, for all intents and purposes, relatively untouched before the meme began. The "rules" of the meme then wrote themselves as more *Downfall* adaptations were made. Ganz's performance was adopted and adapted by thousands of subtitlers who wanted to make Hitler do something else, be something else, react in some other way, be humiliated in a new way, lose the argument, lose his wits, lose the game. Lose the war. Again. In a new way. Through creative subtitling.

PERFORMING SUBTITLES

Subtitling a movie is a skillful art of language translation and timing. Good captions are timed to appear and disappear at the same rate as the speech in the video. Additionally, subtitles should not aim to translate the language word for word, as this is often impossible, but rather to translate the meaning and style of the spoken text. Blogger and subtitler 8thSin states that the subtitler should "fully understand the context of every line, basic story pattern (for consistency), character personalities (for nuance), and the . . . meaning behind what's . . . being said (for context). If you mess up your interpretation, then your translation will be wrong, and your viewers will misinterpret the same way."[13] The process of creative subtitling, with the *Downfall* meme, meanwhile, is both a performance and a learnable skill. While tight and often comedic timing is part of what makes many of the *Downfall* adaptations work, as performance, creative subtitling does not work by translating language well. Instead, the translator works in the realms of non-verbal expression, affect, and cinematography—in everything *but* the literal words. Tone of voice, facial expressions, how the characters move and their use of space and distance, how the characters touch or do not touch each other, the physical appearance and costuming of the characters, and all cinematographic choices (including the distance and angle of the shot, camera movement, and lighting) are interpreted and translated by the creative subtitler. Hitler's extended silence in the often parodied bunker scene, when he shakily removes his glasses in a slightly skewed close-up shot of the side of his face, for example, takes on a new meaning in the context of each adaptation. The silence speaks volumes, and while it is never accompanied by subtitles (in any of the adaptations I've seen, at least), his silence is further explained by the subtitles that proceed and follow it. Generally, the first line he speaks after the silence is something requesting that a large number of people leave the room. In "Hitler Can't See *Avatar*," for example, when he is informed that the movie tickets for *Avatar* are sold out at all of the local theatres, he takes an extended pause, removes his glasses, and states "If you have already seen this film, please leave the room now."[14] Next, after nearly everyone leaves the crowded bunker, Hitler explodes, often swearing at the few remaining officers in outrage and/or disbelief. During this moment in "Hitler Learns He Cannot Divide by Zero," for instance, Hitler yells, "You can't tell me what I can and can't do! I'm Adolf freakin Hitler! When I go to Burger King and order half a frankfurter in my burger, they put half a friggin frankfurter in my burger! So who are you to tell me that I simply can't divide by zero?!"[15] In other videos, the silence is dubbed over with music or crosscut with video clips to contextualize Hitler's response further. In "Hitler Rants About Miley Cyrus," this usually silent moment is underscored with music ("We Can't Stop," by Miley Cyrus), and crosscut with clips from Miley Cyrus's controversial performance at MTV's 2013 Video Music Awards Ceremony. The *Downfall* parody crosscuts between a nearly nude Miley twerking (her risqué "signature" dance), and Hitler, who seems to be staring at her in disgust and disbelief.[16]

Der Untergang is filmed in German. Thus, creative German subtitles would not work in the same way as subtitles in any other language. German subtitles would more likely be interpreted as an intertextual parody of the content of the movie, perhaps showing the characters' thoughts or attempting to say what the characters *really* mean, despite literal interpretations of what they are saying. The possible humor in this type of subtitling would be akin—not aesthetically, but in essence—to how the television show *Mystery Science Theatre 3000* (*MST3K*) works. The major premise of MST3K involves a man and several robot sidekicks who were imprisoned on a space station. The group was forced to watch bad movies (often science fiction or B-movies), as part of a psychological experiment run by an evil scientist. To stay sane, the group provides a running audio commentary while watching the movies. They mock the movie's flaws and inconsistencies, and heckle their way through as if they were in a vaudeville movie theater peanut gallery.

Creative subtitles in any other language besides German do not work on this type of intertextual level, which comments on the content and meaning of the original movie. Instead, creative subtitles in all languages but German offer the possibility of *changing* the content and meaning of the movie, by re-interpreting everything that happens, paying no heed to accurate translation of the language, and giving the chosen scene a totally new context. This type of re-interpretation might be compared to the improvisational game "Film Dub," which was a regular feature on the British (and later American) comedy series *Whose Line Is It Anyway?* To play "Film Dub," up to four performers watch a muted clip from an old and/or unknown movie or television show. While the clip silently plays, the performers improvise a dialogue between the onscreen characters (often following a scene suggestion given to them by the audience or show host). A newer similar online phenomenon, "Bad Lip Readings," reworks clips from movies, television shows, and sports by offering new (and generally silly) voice-overs that closely match what the person on screen seems looks like they are saying. These voice-overs are often funny because they tend toward the absurd and/or nonsensical, and the voices used seem to mock or contradict the physical traits of the person, actor, or known character onscreen (e.g., giving a very large and aggressive football player a high-pitched, whiny voice).

Yet the *Downfall* meme takes the "Film Dub" type of adaptation further, through preplanning and intentionality on the part of the subtitler. Rather than improvised comedy, *Downfall* adaptation subtitles are crafted to fit a scene with which the subtitler is already familiar. While "Bad Lip Readings" often find their humor in the absurdity of trying to visually match what the person onscreen looks like they are saying, the *Downfall* adaptations are freed from this restriction because of their reliance on subtitles. Additionally, while creative subtitlers are working with visual nonverbal cues in the scene, they also have the original actors' particular vocal choices to keep in mind—particularly the breadth of Ganz's vocal performance, which runs a gamut of emotions in under four minutes.

The creatively subtitled versions of *Downfall* begin with a sort of silent "score" (much like a musical score) that needs to be performed to resound. The movie scene, in German, is the score. The scene remains the same, but with each new performance of subtitling, this score that looks and sounds the same with every viewing takes on new meaning. While every *Downfall* adaptation is unique, many of the subtitled versions still share some common elements. In January 2010, Jeremy Hunsinger circulated one of the *Downfall* adaptations to the Association of Internet Researchers mailing list, an international, academic association centered on internet studies. Their mailing list is free, open-access, and includes both members and non-members. After receiving some negative responses, including complaints that the translation was inaccurate and insulting, and that a terrific film had been "ripped off," Hunsinger pointed out that "the clip has nothing to do with Nazis or evil or censorship. The [*Downfall*] meme is playing purely off the emotional portrayals. . . . It is the reproduction and reconstruction of those meanings in relation to the emotions that make this work."[17] Hunsinger advises that, "if you are going to read [this] meme, you should try to do it justice within its own genre."[18]

Alex Leavitt, meanwhile, attempts a structural reading of the narrative of the *Downfall* meme, "without explaining the actual content of the video (since it obviously varies with each parody)."[19] Leavitt offers a relatively simple narrative structure of the scene:

1. An "actor sets up a situation," which his "superior seems to understand."
2. The superior "confirms that he understands."

3. The "actor(s) introduce a problem," that contradicts their superior's understanding.
4. The superior "suggests his frustration in extended silence."
5. The superior "explodes in confused anger."
6. The superior "realizes he cannot overcome problem."
7. The superior "accepts the problem."[20]

According to Leavitt, each *Downfall* meme video "establishes a problem with a (usually hilarious) tirade about a (sometimes banal; occasionally significant) crisis." Regardless of what issue is at stake, the *Downfall* meme "presents a joke (basic meaning) whose structure dictates further meaning when applied to multiple contexts."[21]

Yet, this structural reading is reductive if you intend to take into account the various possible cultural meanings and implications of the creatively subtitled *Downfall* videos. While internet memes are often jokes at first, "they also represent a valuable example of networked knowledge online."[22] Many internet memes are simply humor, and most still remain within "subcultural barriers of small internet communities": those who "get" the joke.[23] But, according to Leavitt, "the evolutionary structure of some memes create[s] a strong cultural value that acts as a grammar for information networks." The value and meaning in acts like creative subtitling (and remix, which I discuss in depth in chapters 2 and 3) does not come from the content of what is said; "it comes from the reference, which is expressible only if it is the original that gets used. Images or sounds collected from real-world examples become 'paint on a palette.'"[24] It is the "'cultural reference,' as coder and remix artist Victor Stone explained, that 'has emotional meaning to people.'"[25]

Creative subtitling may also be considered a learned skill (through a sort of *techno-play*) for future humorous and/or video-based communications. Stanford Law Professor Lawrence Lessig considers how literacies in newer media are understood, in an historical context, and in relation to writing:

> While writing with text is the stuff that everyone is taught to do, filmmaking and record making were, for most of the twentieth century, the stuff that professionals did. That meant it was easier to imagine a regime that required permission to quote with film and music. Such a regime was at least feasible, even if inefficient. But what happens when writing with film (or music, or images, or every other form of 'professional speech' from the twentieth century) becomes as democratic as writing with text?[26]

Lessig goes on to compare current day text "writing" (versus other mediated ways of communicating) to Latin, in the Middle Ages in Europe. "Text is today's Latin"; an elite, and relatively inaccessible, skill. The masses in the Middle Ages in Europe did not speak Latin. They spoke "local, or vernacular, languages—what we now call French, German, and

English."[27] Thus, "the most 'important' texts were understood by only a few." Elites now communicate through text, while most people, according to Lessig, gather information through "TV, film, music, and music video. These forms of 'writing' are the vernacular of today. They are the kinds of 'writing' that matters most to most."[28] In the future, the skill of creative subtitling may prove useful for further creative political engagement, particularly for those who enjoy receiving and forwarding their news ironically (e.g., those who enjoyed *The Colbert Report*, watch *The Daily Show*, or pay attention to the many news-related memes that plaster personal feeds on Facebook, Twitter, and other social networking sites every day).

At the same time, video-making is not "writing," and it requires a different set of skills. A number of instructional videos, many made by Untergangers, explain how to make a "good" *Downfall* parody to new creators. Several videos walk viewers through the entire process of downloading, subtitling, finalizing their files, and uploading the video to YouTube. Some videos even give suggestions about subtitles: for example, place text near the bottom of the screen, keep text flowing at the same pace as the actor's speech, don't fade text in or out, avoid all caps writing, use white text, and a use a readable, non-script font. Other videos offer more general advice, like double-checking spelling and grammar and using swear words liberally.[29] Through "Hitler and His Friends Explain How to Make a PROPER Hitler Parody," for instance, the viewer learns to "make sure your subtitles follow the emotions of the audio . . . and if you think it's a ranting feeling, put in an exclamation mark!"[30]

In one video, the subtitler (through Hitler) even teaches others how to cut and edit scenes, dub audio over existing clips, and properly match the chosen punctuation to the emotion of the scene. Hitler then advises subtitlers on what video editing programs they should be using, including Windows Movie Maker, Corel VideoStudio 12, and Sony Vegas. He then exclaims, "[I]f you own a Mac, you have to use Final Cut Pro! Required! Never use iMovie!"[31] This advice has to do with the subtitle functions on iMovie and Final Cut. iMovie, according to this video maker, is much more difficult to work with, in terms of syncing text well with speech.

Another instructional video uses a clip from a different scene in *Downfall*, which does not even include Hitler, to stage an exchange between the prolific video-maker "Hitler Rants Parodies" (HRP, who has made over 1,400 Downfall parodies), and some novice creators. In this scene, HRP confronts the rookie subtitlers, several Hitler Youth members, on the street. The youngsters use awkward fonts, the fade-in and fade-out text functions, and have terrible spelling and grammar. HRP attempts to teach them the technical nuances of making a video that people will enjoy watching. The younger creators, however, resist his advice, and ultimately seem ignorant and closed-minded, in comparison to HRP.[32]

Regardless of how "good" or "proper" any given adaptation is, as Lessig points out, this type of creative activity produces two goods: community and education. According to Lessig, who focuses on remix culture, the creative activity of remix happens within a community: "Members of that community create in part for one another. They are showing one another how they can create, as kids on a skateboard are showing their friends how they can create. That showing is valuable, even when the stuff produced is not."[33] Just as there is good and bad writing, there are good and bad remixes. "But just as bad writing is not an argument against writing, bad remix is not an argument against remix. Instead, in both cases, poor work is an argument for better education."[34] Finally, in the response to the criticism that "remix is just crap," Lessig states that while this may be true, the critic that brings this up is missing the point. The vast majority of any art is "just crap," with products that are "silly," "derivative," and even "a waste of . . . the creator's time, let alone the consumer's."[35] The value and meaning for the remixer lies as much, if not more, in the process of remixing as it does in any final product.

GATEKEEPING, INSIDE JOKES, META-PARODIES, AND TECHNO-PLAY

Similar to how Lessig describes the value and meaning of remixing, for some creative subtitlers, the value and meaning of their work lies in their connection to the *Untergangers* community and internet meme communities in general, along with the personal identity performances, inside jokes, and positive in-group feelings that belonging to these communities allows. A number of the subtitled videos, for example, offer inside jokes, internet jokes, and various fan jokes and commentaries. Since his first reaction in 2006, which was about a video game, Hitler has reacted to nearly every videogame system release, along with many individual game releases. Hitler has reacted to being Rickrolled, the "2 Girls 1 Cup" video, the antics of Kanye West, "Gangnam Style," Susan Boyle, and Rebecca Black's infamous music video, "Friday." Hitler has also ranted about *Star Trek*, Where's Waldo, finding out Pokémon are not real, the Pokémon Go game, a tea pot advertisement in which the teapot vaguely looks like Hitler, and both Hillary Clinton and Donald Trump's presidential campaigns. Further, Hitler continues to react to the deaths of popular musicians and actors; in 2016, these reactions included his response to the passing of David Bowie, Prince, Alan Rickman, and Gene Wilder, among others. This list barely scratches the surface of the thousands of cultural happenings and popular and political culture phenomena about which Hitler has found out, and to which Hitler has reacted. A Google search of "Hitler reacts to [fill in the popular culture reference of your choice]" is nearly guaranteed to produce at least one video result.[36]

With each of these videos, the viewer must be a least vaguely familiar with the popular culture phenomenon in question to get the joke. Thus, these videos act as a sort of gate-keeping mechanism for various subcultures. Individuals and communities can use these videos to associate themselves with specific groups, actively build personal identities, form or maintain interpersonal relationships, and create social contexts. Meanwhile, they are also implicitly creating their own hierarchies and rules about who does and does not fit in. If a viewer doesn't get the joke just by reading the title, she is probably less likely to watch the video. If she does watch the video, and finds it funny or intriguing, this viewer might do some research into the pop culture reference, to understand better and/or associate herself with the target/ideal audience of the *Downfall* adaptation she watched.

Some adaptations that demonstrate the use of creative subtitling also seem to be techno-play videos. These videos experiment with different scenes in the movie (i.e., not the four-minute bunker scene), and with video editing technology, as part of the joke. One video uses a mirroring effect to show how Hitler has been informed that there are multiple Hitlers.[37] Other videos add different special effects, images, and/or music. In one video, Hitler looks like he is eating Cheetos; in another he pushes a lit cartoon bomb off of his table; in yet another he is listening and reacting to dubstep, a genre of dance music that is stylistically influenced by broken beat, drum and bass, jungle, and reggae music. Few of these videos demonstrate technical expertise on the part of the creator(s), yet this does not stop the creators from experimenting with video editing technology and sharing their results publicly on YouTube. Adapters are inspired by this meme, enough so to play around with video technologies, and they are potentially learning how to use said technologies as they create. Even more than creative subtitling, proficiency in video editing is an incredibly valuable skill that can be useful in many personal, social, professional, and educational settings.

The *Downfall* video meme also includes a large number of meta-memes, in which Hitler reacts to the "Hitler reacts to" video meme. Indeed, Hitler has even been informed that he is not in fact Hitler, but is Bruno Ganz.[38] Meanwhile, a twisted reflection of this sentiment crops up in another video, which depicts Bruno Ganz reacting to the *Downfall* meme. In "Hitler Actor Bruno Ganz Interview about YouTube Downfall Parodies," Ganz, who "put everything into this performance" can't escape being Hitler. Even still, Ganz expresses how impressed he is by the creativity put into all of the *Downfall* adaptations. Ganz states that he is just happy that "everyone is enjoying themselves, that's all that matters, really. In fact, they've made me more popular than I could ever imagine." While it seems like a legitimate interview at first, those familiar with the *Downfall* meme might recognize the video parody for what it is around the time that Ganz begins speaking about putting "the smack down" on his wife and kids for making fun of him.[39] The video is actually a creatively subtitled parody of a behind the scenes interview, of Bruno Ganz talking about the making of *Downfall.* In the comments section of the video, German speakers who seem unfamiliar with the meme complain about how inaccurate the subtitles are and demand that the video be taken down. They, like others who are not "in" on the *Downfall* joke, are missing the point of this creatively subtitled extension of the *Downfall* meme. Those who are familiar with the *Downfall* video meme, meanwhile, gear up to hear what Bruno Ganz thinks about the whole phenomenon. Eventually, though—while watching, reading comments, or discussing the video—these *Downfall* meme followers realize that the joke is on them. The video is like a behind-the-scenes look at the *Downfall* meme, made in the form and spirit of the *Downfall* meme. After realizing the video is creatively subtitled, it seems obvious: of course Bruno Ganz's children don't point and laugh at him and ask if he's found and killed Fegelein yet! In fact, a quick Wikipedia search reveals that Ganz only has one adult son who has been blind since the age of four—a son well beyond the age of pointing and laughing, who is not capable of reading the non-German subtitles on the YouTube videos, which he would need to do to understand much of the humor of the meme.

Finally, this meme shows how the process of subtitling can be a form of cultural play. Julie Cohen notes that "play," in the realm of remix culture, means intentional activity by individual creators, along with the "flex" in cultural practices of representation. "'Play of culture' is the result of the complex intersection of consumption, communications, self-development and creative (intentional) play."[40] Many *Downfall* video adaptations not only play with culture, but also attempt to make explicit cultural and political statements. Hitler has reacted to the Penn State scandal, rising tuition costs at colleges and universities, Mitt Romney's loss to Barack Obama, cyberbullying, gay marriage, the EU Referendum result, and multiple presidential campaigns in the United States. Again, this is just the tip of the *Downfall* adaptation iceberg.

Beyond these, many adaptations address current issues regarding internet censorship, and generally depict Hitler reacting negatively to censorship. The Stop Online Piracy Act (SOPA), for example, was a bill introduced into US Congress in October, 2011, with the intent of protecting the intellectual property market and strengthening the enforcement of copyright laws. Hitler's many reactions to SOPA pointed to the negative effects the bill could have on online communities that host user-generated content, like YouTube. SOPA had broad support from a number of organizations that rely on copyright, including the Motion Picture Association of America, the Recording Industry Association of America, Entertainment Software Association, Macmillan US, Viacom, along with other companies in the cable, movie, and music industries. Yet, many online communities and networks—like YouTube users—responded negatively to the bill. Hitler thus moseyed his way into said networks via the *Downfall* meme. In one anti-SOPA video, Hitler even accuses the US Congress and the businesses that supported SOPA of wanting to "cripple the only medium that's consistently creating jobs and growth." In this video, Hitler continues his rant, stating, "you don't get to destroy the internet because it doesn't fit your business model!" Meanwhile, the woman consoling another crying woman in the hallway, halfway through the video, states, "Don't cry. Disney owns the rights to that emotion."[41]

COPYRIGHT, FAIR USE, AND THE "STREISAND EFFECT"

The *Downfall* meme has had its own run-ins with copyright law, making it relevant to issues of copyright, fair use, and the "Streisand effect." In April 2010, producers and German distributors Constantin Films, using YouTube's Content ID system, began requesting the removal of *Downfall* parodies from YouTube. Such an attempt to censor specific online information can attract unwanted attention, and the "Streisand Effect" is a type of public backlash against internet censorship. Rather than being successfully removed from the public sphere, the information in question becomes more widely available than it was before the censorship attempt. The term was coined after Barbara Streisand, in 2003, unsuccessfully sued photographer Kenneth Adelman and Pictopia.com, hoping to have an aerial photograph of her home removed from a public collection of 12,000 photos of California's coast. Before Streisand's lawsuit, the image of her home had been downloaded six times. Because of the case, public knowledge of the photo grew, and within a month more than 420,000 people visited Aldeman's website to view the photo.[42]

Constantin's removal of *Downfall* parodies caused a similar backlash among YouTube users, who put many of the removed videos back up, made more videos, and made *Downfall* adaptations specifically about the Constantin takedown. One video shows Hitler's inevitable reaction to the Hitler adaptations being removed from YouTube, as he rants that "Nobody uploading a video to YouTube has the money to defend themselves in a copyright infringement lawsuit!" In this same video, Hitler shows off his knowledge of US Copyright Law and Fair Use, as he asks, "Haven't they ever heard of Fair Use? Title 17, U.S.C., Section 107?"[43] Many YouTube users adamantly fought Constantin's takedown request, claiming that fair use laws protected their videos as parodies. Meanwhile, during the wave of takedowns, several parodists had their videos blocked, while others had their accounts suspended. Some creators deleted parodies that they had made to prevent their YouTube channels from being suspended. In October 2010, six months after the initial takedown initiative, "Constantin, instead of blocking videos, placed [advertisements] on parodies instead. Downfall videos that were previously blocked, were back on YouTube. . . . [Yet,] while previously blocked parodies . . . were unblocked, videos that parodists deleted because of the copyright takedowns were gone."[44] Constantin has yet to release any official statement about its change in policy, in regards to the takedowns of the YouTube parodies.

The network of YouTube users that make these video parodies are learning about and teaching each other their legal rights, in terms of what texts they can and cannot use in their videos, and why. Groups have formed with the explicit purpose of educating the online video-making masses about copyright law. The Institute for Internet Studies, for example, created a public service announcement explaining how to dispute a wrongful copyright claim on the grounds of fair use. Meanwhile, in 2016, there are *still* sketchy legal distinctions between "satire," which is *not* permissible in regard to copyright law, and "parody," which *can be* considered under Fair Use. According to Juli Wilson Marshall and Nicholas J. Siciliano:

> One explanation rooted in the First Amendment for the disparate treatment of parody versus satire is that while a copyright owner might be understandably wary of licensing a criticism or ridicule of his own work (a parody), he might be willing to license his work as a vehicle for broader social comment. . . . Put another way . . . while a scathing parody may destroy the market for the original work, its destruction stems from criticism, not usurpation by acting as a substitute. In addition, even if a copyright owner refuses to license a satirical use of the work, it is arguable that a pure satire still should not be considered a fair use, considering a satire benefits from the popularity of the original work and is more likely to act as a market substitute.[45]

While this parody/satire distinction has become central to many fair use cases, "the proper dividing line between quintessential parody and satire is blurry at best" and "creative lawyers and judges have taken advantage of this blurriness in arguing for (or against) the parodic character of works."[46] Lessig, meanwhile, explains that what Hollywood is worried about is not necessarily making money off of satires, parodies or remixes, but rather its own reputation: i.e., *What if a clip gets misused? What if Nazis spin it on their website?* According to Lessig, this problem stems from the law having *too much* control, rather than not enough: "Because the law allows the copyright owner to veto use, the copyright owner must worry about misuse." Lessig suggests that the solution to this worry is less power: "If the owner can't control the use, then the misuse is not the owner's responsibility."[47] In his book, *Free Culture,* Lessig also explains some of the paradoxes of "fair use":

> In theory, fair use means you need no permission. The theory therefore supports free culture and insulates against a permission culture. But in

> practice, fair use functions very differently. The fuzzy lines of the law, tied to the extraordinary liability if lines are crossed, means that the effective fair use for many types of creators is slight. The law has the right aim; practice has defeated the aim. . . . The law was born as a shield to protect publishers' profits against the unfair competition of a pirate. It has matured into a sword that interferes with any use, transformative or not.[48]

In the end, these cases are up to court ruling, on a case-by-case basis. Yet, the larger scope of the meme shows how attempted censorship of creative public performances can result in a creative public backlash, and call attention to rigid or vague laws (like fair use and copyright) that may not serve the interests of the publics for whom they are supposedly in place.

Lessig also discusses how creativity is subject to regulation, by default, for the first time in history. While cultural objects or products created digitally can be easily copied, the default copyright law requires the permission of the owner. A creator needs the permission of the copyright owner to make a remix of the content, or to adapt the content in any way. What we now call "piracy" has not always been a shameful crime, and has even benefited creative industries in the past. According to Lessig, "[i]f 'piracy' means using value from someone else's creative property without permission from that creator—as it is increasingly described today—then every industry affected by copyright today is the product and beneficiary of a certain kind of piracy. Film, records, radio, cable TV. . . . Every generation welcomes the pirates from the last. Every generation—until now."[49]

Balances between new technologies, methods of content distribution, and the law, and balance between the rights of creators and the protection of innovation, has been the history of the US content industry; not "zero tolerance" for re-using others' work.[50] Copyright in 1710, for example, "was born as a very specific set of restrictions: It forbade others from reprinting a book."[51] Today, however, copyright has expanded to include "a large collection of restrictions on the freedom of others: It grants the author the exclusive right to copy, the exclusive right to distribute, the exclusive right to perform, and so on."[52] Copyright now also protects derivative rights: "The copyright, in other words, is now not just an exclusive right to your writings, but an exclusive right to your writings and a large proportion of the writings inspired by them."[53] Additionally, Lessig points out that "there is no check on silly rules" on the internet, because rules online are often enforced by machines rather than humans: "Increasingly," Lessig states, "the rules of copyright law, as interpreted by the copyright owner, get built into the technology that delivers copyrighted content. It is code, rather than law, that rules. And the problem with code regulations is that, unlike law, code has no shame. Code would not get the humor of the Marx Brothers. The consequence of that is not at all funny."[54]

YouTube, for example, uses a database system called Content ID, in which are stored millions of video and audio files ("reference files") that copyright holders may want YouTube to "look for" on the site.[55] Every time a video is uploaded to YouTube, Content ID compares it to every reference file in the database, looking for audio matches, video matches, and partial matches. When the program finds a match, it does whatever the copyright holder has requested be done to that video, including blocking the video so it cannot be viewed, tracking the video so the copyright owner can see "how many views the video receives and from where," muting the audio on the video, or advertising on the video and giving monetary compensation to the copyright owner.[56] Yet, Content ID does not have any way of determining fair use. In the case Lenz v. Universal, for example, the Electronic Frontier Foundation sued Universal Music Group for taking down a short home video of a baby dancing to a Prince song on YouTube; "[C]ourts ordered that rights holders had to consider fair use before issuing a takedown notice."[57] Thus, while Content ID might work on a mass scale for YouTube and copyright holders, it is easy to imagine the many cases where videos that would be considered fair use by a human being are removed, muted, tracked, or advertised on, because computers can't register the nuances of parody and complicities of fair use.

Finally, Lessig reminds us that all creative property has more than one life. In the first life of a very small number of creative works, the content may be sold ("if the creator is lucky"), and in these cases "the commercial market is successful for the creator."[58] However, after this first life has ended, there is a second life for such works. Lessig offers the example of a newspaper, which "delivers the news every day to the doorsteps of America" and the next day "is used to wrap fish or to fill boxes with fragile gifts or to build an archive of knowledge about our history. In this second life, the content can continue to inform even if that information is no longer sold."[59] Despite this type of noncommercial cycling of knowledge and creativity, we have a "system of technology that invites [us] to be creative," and "a system of law [that] prevents [us] from creating legally."[60] In addition to pointing out problematic copyright laws, Lessig posits that we need to "reset our norms" to fit the time we live in, as "[o]ur norms and expectations around the control of culture have been set by a century that was radically different from the century we're in. . . . We need to develop a set of judgments about how to react appropriately to speech that we happen not to like. We, as a society, need to develop and deploy these norms."[61] The law and/or its interpretation, then, may eventually catch up with the norm.

The *Downfall* meme inspired a recent step in this general direction. In Dec. 2010, JPMorgan employee Grant Williams was fired for sharing a *Downfall* parody with his coworkers over company email. In June 2013, Deputy High Court Judge Conrad Seagroatt ruled that Williams "shouldn't have been blamed for the Dec. 7, 2010 newsletter."[62] The letter included a link to a *Downfall* parody, with subtitles that mocked JPMorgan Chase & Co. Chief Executive Officer Jamie Dimon. The ruling stated that Williams' "firing the next day for unacceptable conduct was 'hypersensitive' and 'irrational.'"[63] Williams was awarded $1.86 million.

According to *Huffington Post* writer Jason Linkins, "The widespread proliferation of these [*Downfall* adaptation] videos has, over time, reduced their cultural potency in accordance with the laws of diminishing returns. This is what makes Grant Williams' court rendered windfall so exciting. I doubt you'd find anyone who made seven figures pursuing some sort of Downfall meme-related activity."[64] Yet, I believe this court ruling does just the opposite. The ruling shows the increased (rather than reduced) cultural potency of these videos. "Financial potency" may have been better wording for what Linkins seems to be saying. However, concern with the financial potency of the *Downfall* adaptations misses the point. People clearly want to make *statements* with their *Downfall* adaptations, regardless of whether or not they ever make *money* from said adaptations. This court ruling may be proof that, as cultural practices of video adaptation are becoming normalized, the ways that laws are being interpreted are starting to catch up with the video adapting masses.

Meanwhile, the case Schmidt v. Warner Bros. created a stir in terms of the ownership and copyright of internet memes, that—while a legitimate move for the plaintiffs—seems a step backwards in terms of public understanding of both how memes work and what they are. According to Rachel Weber of Games Industry International, "The creators of popular memes Keyboard Cat and Nyan Cat have filed a copyright and trademark infringement lawsuit against Warner Bros. and 5th Cell Media over their characters' appearances in the *Scribblenauts* games. Christopher Orlando Torres and Charles Schmidt's complaint says the memes were used in *Scribblenauts* products without their permission."[65] Torres states, about Warner Bros. use of Nyan Cat, "I have no issues with Nyan Cat being enjoyed by millions of fans as a meme, and I have never tried to prevent people from making creative uses of it that contribute artistically and are not for profit. But this is a commercial use, and these companies themselves are protectors of their own intellectual property."[66] While Torres's point is valid, in terms of commercial versus noncommercial uses, his definition of meme misses the mark. Torres and Schmidt did not create *memes*. They created videos involving "Keyboard Cat" (a live cat playing a keyboard) and "Nyan Cat" (a cartoon character with a cat's face and a body that looks like a pink Pop Tart, that flies across the screen with a rainbow trailing behind it). These two videos became memes because of the actions of a large number of other people, but they did not begin as such. The plaintiffs may have more accurately sued, and rightly so, about the copyright of these characters, rather than the copyright of the memes. This distinction is incredibly important. The meme is not a static thing; it is not some original video, but rather all the variations, copies, and adaptations of a video, as well as the cultural forces that move and spread the video, inspiring many others to create and share alike.

Hitler's reaction to Nyan Cat, meanwhile, was predictable. After he shakily removed his glasses and sent most of the group out of the bunker, he screamed the few who remained in the room: "How dare they make a flying fucking poptart cat!? I was going to make a flying-toast cat. And they dare steal my ideas with their shit-flavored poptarts!!"[67]

NOTES

1. Andy Nordvall, "Hitler Is Fed Up with All the Hitler Rants!" YouTube, Mar. 15, 2009, accessed July 25, 2012, https://www.youtube.com/watch?v=7vMUvgce_5s.
2. *Downfall.* Dir. Hirschbiegel, Oliver. Perf. Bruno Ganz. Constantine Films, 2004.
3. A YouTube search of "Hitler reacts to" brings up more than 1.2 million results, as of October 22, 2016.
4. Nordvall, "Hitler Is Fed Up."
5. "Downfall Parodies Forum," accessed Aug. 31, 2016, http://www.downfallparodies.net/forum/.
6. O'Flynn, "Epilogue," loc. 3800.
7. Siobhan O'Flynn, "Epilogue," in Linda Hutcheon's *A Theory of Adaptation* (London: Routledge, 2012), Kindle edition, loc. 3854.
8. GubraeTheSecond, "Hitler Gets Rick Rolled," YouTube, May 6, 2009, accessed June 5, 2013, https://www.youtube.com/watch?v=LLd2uAam0hI.
9. Virginia Heffernan, "The Hitler Meme," *The New York Times Magazine*, Oct. 24, 2008, accessed July 26, 2012, http://www.nytimes.com/2008/10/26/magazine/26wwln-medium-t.html?_r=0.
10. Emma Rosenblum, "The Director of *Downfall* Speaks Out on All Those Angry YouTube Hitlers," Vulture, *nymag.com*, Jan. 15, 2010, accessed July 21, 2013, http://www.vulture.com/2010/01/the_director_of_downfall_on_al.html.
11. Rosenblum, "The Director of *Downfall*."
12. Heffernan, "The Hitler Meme."
13. 8thSin, "Fan Translation Guide," *8thSin Fansubs Anime Blog*, Mar. 18, 2012, accessed Oct. 13, 2013 (blog has been removed from the internet).
14. Andrew Hagerman, "Hitler Can't See Avatar," YouTube, Feb. 5, 2010, accessed Oct. 13, 2013, https://www.youtube.com/watch?v=j32qsBHS0b8.
15. DrMathRSA's channel, "Hitler Learns He Cannot Divide by Zero," YouTube, Aug. 23, 2010, accessed Oct. 13, 2013, https://www.youtube.com/watch?v=FuTz3NL32AM.
16. Soalric Parker, "Hitler Rants About Miley Cyrus," YouTube, Aug. 27, 2013, accessed Oct. 13, 2013, https://www.youtube.com/watch?v=iYZRsL6ie4A.
17. Jeremy Hunsinger, as quoted in Alex Leavitt, "Memes as Mechanisms: How Digital Subculture Informs the Real World," *Futures of Entertainment*, Feb. 2, 2010, accessed July 21 2010, http://www.convergenceculture.org/weblog/2010/02/memes_as_mechanisms_how_digita.php.
18. Leavitt, "Memes as Mechanisms."
19. Leavitt, "Memes as Mechanisms."
20. Leavitt, "Memes as Mechanisms."
21. Leavitt, "Memes as Mechanisms."
22. Leavitt, "Memes as Mechanisms."
23. Leavitt, "Memes as Mechanisms."
24. Lawrence Lessig, *Remix: Making Art and Commerce Thrive in the Hybrid Economy* (New York: Penguin Group, 2010), Kindle edition, loc. 1632–37.

25. Victor Stone as quoted in Lessig, *Remix,* loc. 1640–41.
26. Lessig, *Remix,* loc. 1240–48.
27. Lessig, *Remix* loc. 1507–17.
28. Lessig, *Remix* loc. 1507–17.
29. For example, 555ReactionTime, "Hitler and Friends Explain How to Make a Hitler Parody," YouTube, Jan. 2, 2012, accessed July 23, 2013, https://www.youtube.com/watch?v=198E05RJV5o; avidsonicfan1991, "Hitler and His Friends Explain How to Make a PROPER Hitler Parody," YouTube, Sept. 25, 2012, accessed July 25, 2013 (video has been removed from YouTube); Hitler Rants Parodies, "Hitler Plans to Make a Downfall Parody," YouTube, Mar. 29, 2010, accessed May 19, 2013, https://www.youtube.com/watch?v=ua0bniu-aMA.
30. avidsonicfan1991, "Hitler and His Friends Explain."
31. avidsonicfan1991, "Hitler and His Friends Explain."
32. Hitler Rants Parodies, "Hitler Plans to Make."
33. Lessig, *Remix,* loc. 1669–83.
34. Lessig, *Remix,* loc. 1763–68.
35. Lessig, *Remix,* loc. 1959–65.
36. As of August 2016.
37. Hitler Rants, Parodies, "Hitler Is Informed That There Are Two Hitlers," YouTube, June 27, 2010, accessed July 21, 2013, https://www.youtube.com/watch?v=LP12x81uYDU.
38. Hitler Rants Parodies, "Hitler is informed he is Bruno Ganz," YouTube, Feb. 24, 2010, accessed July 21, 2013, https://www.youtube.com/watch?v=SB7hYC3lWa8.
39. Amp, "Hitler Actor Bruno Ganz Interview about Youtube Downfall Parodies," YouTube, Feb. 21, 2012, accessed May 19, 2013, https://www.youtube.com/watch?v=4YLqC3DIgjY.
40. Julie E. Cohen, "The Place of the User in Copyright Law," *Fordham Law Review* 74 (2005), 373.
41. FightingInternet, "Hitler Reacts to SOPA," YouTube, Dec. 20, 2011, accessed July 21, 2013, https://www.youtube.com/watch?v=uvXo4sGB7zM.
42. Paul Rogers, "Streisand's Home Becomes Hit on Web," *San Jose Mercury News,* June 24, 2003.
43. Plankhead, "Hitler Reacts to the Hitler Parodies Being Removed from YouTube," YouTube, Apr. 20, 2010, accessed June 19, 2013, https://www.youtube.com/watch?v=kBO5dh9qrIQ.
44. "History of Downfall Parodies," *Hitler Parody Wiki,* accessed Oct. 13, 2013, http://hitlerparody.wikia.com/wiki/History_of_Downfall_parodies.
45. Juli Wilson Marshall and Nicholas J. Siciliano, "The Satire/Parody Distinction in Copyright and Trademark Law—Can Satire Ever Be a Fair Use?" ABA Section of Litigation, Intellectual Property Litigation Committee Roundtable Discussion Online, PDF, accessed July 16, 2012, https://apps.americanbar.org/litigation/committees/intellectual/roundtables/0506_outline.pdf.
46. Marshall and Siciliano, "The Satire/Parody Distinction," 4.
47. Lessig, *Remix* loc. 5039–60.
48. Lawrence Lessig, *Free Culture: How Big Media Uses Technology and the Law to Lock Down Culture and Control Creativity* (New York: Penguin Group, 2004), Kindle edition, loc. 1287–95.
49. Lessig, *Free Culture,* loc. 843–46.
50. Lessig, *Free Culture,* loc. 1012–15.
51. Lessig, *Free Culture,* loc. 1145–50.
52. Lessig, *Free Culture,* loc. 1145–50.
53. Lessig, *Free Culture,* loc. 1766–70.
54. Lessig, *Free Culture,* loc. 1879–82.
55. As of May 2014.

56. Christina Warren, "How YouTube Fights Copyright Infringement," *Mashable,* Feb. 17, 2012, accessed Oct. 13, 2013, http://mashable.com/2012/02/17/youtube-content-id-faq/#0pPsfN6AD5qa.
57. Warren, "How YouTube Fights."
58. Lessig, *Remix,* loc. 1458–66.
59. Lessig, *Remix,* loc. 1458–66.
60. Lessig, *Remix,* loc. 5236–71.
61. Lessig, *Remix,* loc. 5378–5407.
62. Bei Hu, "Jefferies Must Pay Fired Trader $1.86 Million, Court Says," *Bloomberg,* July 8, 2013.
63. Hu, "Jefferies Must Pay."
64. Jason Linkins, "The 'Downfall' Internet Meme Has FINALLY Made Somebody Rich," *The Huffington Post,* July 9, 2013, accessed July 21, 2013, http://www.huffingtonpost.com/2013/07/09/downfall-internet-meme_n_3568221.html.
65. Rachel Weber, "Cat Meme Creators in Legal Battle with Scribblenauts," *GamesIndustry International,* May 3, 2013, accessed Oct. 13, 2013, http://www.gamesindustry.biz/articles/2013-05-03-cat-meme-creators-in-legal-battle-with-scribblenauts.
66. Weber, "Cat meme."
67. Alerion, "Hitler's Reaction to the Nyan Cat (Hitler Parody)," YouTube, June 1, 2011, accessed Oct. 14, 2013, https://www.youtube.com/watch?v=tDolSn3Xvzc.

FIVE

Sweding *Dirty Harry*: Collaged Confessions of a Cinemasochist

It's a Friday afternoon, and I'm gathering costumes and props, scripts, and writing out a shooting schedule. I glance around my living room. The array of objects on my floor, couches, and coffee table makes me laugh: a frumpy pink dress, a stuffed monkey, a leather wallet, three squirt guns, two aluminum foil police badges, five wigs, toy binoculars, four ugly neckties, an old typewriter case, medical tape, bandages, a ski mask I made by cutting eye and mouth holes into a pink winter hat, a red sweater, a few packets of ketchup, a denim shirt, paper plates, a green rotary phone, a wooden crate, sunglasses, toilet paper, a stapler, a black sharpie, and a Sony Flip™ camera. On my porch, there is a "school bus" I made out of a table, five chairs, fifteen stuffed animals, an orange travel towel, and some electrical tape. I have all of the trashy makings to shoot a crappy movie. But I won't be shooting a movie; I'll be *sweding* a movie. I look at my trash with pride and excitement, and take a picture of some of it to post to my Facebook page, with the caption "just a coffee table" and a winking emoticon.

While producers of "sweded" movies do not always use digital technologies to make their videos, they bridge the off/online binary by using digital media and online social networking sites to disseminate their low-tech videos, and to watch the sweded movies others have made. The terms "sweded" and "sweding" were first used in Michel Gondry's movie *Be Kind Rewind* (2008), as terms pertaining to the process of remaking popular movies on a shoe-string budget.[1] Aesthetically, and often in terms of intentionality, sweding waffles between homage, burlesque, and pastiche, and sweded cinema aesthetics are akin to "amateur" video, home video, grade-Z movies, and low-budget theatre. Sweding could be considered a form of play, where "play is at the heart of experimentation . . . [and] playing has no stated purpose other than more play."[2] Sweding can also be a way to practice and develop complex, creative and technical skills like video camera use, storyboarding, and film directing.

These practices and skills all work on a larger cultural scale, through what Paul Connerton terms "inscribing" and "incorporating" practices, allowing a person or group to use media (in this case, video) to make a place for him/her/themselves within popular culture(s) and digital networks or communities.[3] According to Connerton, we "re-enact" the past through our bodily performances, using two types of practices. Incorporating practices include social activities where the body is present and doing an activity (e.g., working a video camera). The person engaging in the *doing* is both creating and sustaining bodily memories. Connerton uses the example of how posture is learned and reproduced in cultures to express power and rank, and then the power structure is reinforced through "verbal conventions" (e.g., "upright" meaning honest, just and loyal).[4] With inscribing practices, meanwhile, the body does not have to be present for memories to be stored and retrieved. Rather, these memories are kept by some non-human object (e.g., a book or photograph), which can "trap and hold" information.[5] Video is another medium that might preserve inscriptions—both the actions of the camera operator and those on the video.

Movie sweders are situated in a tangled web of inseparable inscribing and incorporating practices: they are using pre-existing movies (inscribed by others), to create their own versions of said movies through incorporating practices, like set and costume construction, film directing, acting, and camera work. Capturing their video and uploading it online for others to watch is another inscribing practice. They are partaking in a cycle of using and re-creating what Robin Bernstein would call "scriptive things."[6] Video-to-video adaptations (including sweded videos, but also more generally) can be compared to Bernstein's concept of the "scriptive thing," which, like a play script, "broadly structures a performance while allowing for agency, and unleashing original, live variations that may not be individually predictable." Bernstein explains:

> The heuristic of the scriptive thing explodes the very model of archive and repertoire as distinct but interactive, because the word 'script' captures the moment when dramatic narrative and movement through space are in the act of becoming each other. . . . Within each scriptive thing, archive and repertoire are one. Therefore, when scriptive things enter a repository, repertoires arrive with them. Within a brick-and-mortar archive, scriptive things archive the repertoire—partially and richly, with a sense of openness and flux. To read things as scripts is to coax the archive into divulging the repertoire.[7]

At the same time, the incorporating and inscribing practices involved in sweding videos do not necessarily reinforce past values and power structures. Video-makers are *changing the script* of the scriptive things they use and create. Additionally, following Nicolas Bourriaud's theories about postproduction, the creators of sweded movies see contemporary works of art (i.e., Hollywood films) not as a "termination point in the 'creative process'" or a "finished product to be contemplated," but rather as "a site of navigation, a portal, [and] a generator" for new creation(s).[8] As Bourriaud states, even an intended "shot-for-shot remake" is dealing with something different than the "original work," as actors, location, and shifts in sociocultural context will inevitably show how time has passed.[9] Sweded movies take this idea at face value, explicitly calling attention to how time that has passed, and how one might see a previously popular Hollywood movie *now*. These short, amateur-ish, low budget, sweded video adaptations thus give viewers a new way to look at Hollywood movies—through the eyes of other Hollywood movie *viewers*. Full-length movies are condensed into two-to-eight-minute movies. Generally, sweders use parts of the movie that are well known and/or the parts that they like best. The narrative of the film is sometimes lost altogether, in favor of sweding key scenes that may not create a cohesive story for someone who has never seen the original movie. Finally, costumes, set, and special effects in sweded movies are celebrated for their creativity (in terms of remaking professional movie aesthetics with cheap arts and crafts), and their cheesiness. Attempts at realism and suspension of disbelief make for a sub-par sweded movie. Sweders know their audience: themselves, family and friends, and anyone who chooses to watch their movie online, knowing that it is sweded—because it's labeled that way or it's on a website that is devoted to sweded movies.

In this chapter, I weave together several interrelated threads: a non-exhaustive historical precedence for sweded cinema, descriptions and analyses of some popular sweded videos, and a personal account of the process of sweding the movie *Dirty Harry* (1971). I explain how sweded cinema—as digital adaptation—is not unique to the digital age or digital technology. Combining Deb Margolin's ideas about parody, and extending J. Hoberman's theories about the "cinemasochistic" film audience to include cinemasochistic performers, I explain how sweded cinema thrives when performers and audiences are equally invested in the creation and appreciation of "bad" art. Sweded movies are at once *bad* art for art's sake, a lampoon of big-budget Hollywood filmmaking norms, and often a highly social endeavor.

BAD CINEMA AND THE CINEMASOCHIST

Some moviemakers value the process of creation and production, despite the product. Big Budget Hollywood, however, has always been product-oriented. By the 1920s, the "Big Five" film studios—20th Century Fox,

RKO, Paramount Pictures, Warner Bros and MGM—were all located in southern California and had a firm control of the film industry. These studios used vertical integration systems, controlling every aspect of the industry from production to distribution. Additionally, "systems like block booking and blind-buying were employed by these big studios; practices which kept smaller companies and independent productions from gaining a firm foothold in the national film industry."[10] The Big Five did so until 1948's Paramount Decree made these practices illegal. After the Paramount Decree, newer independent studios started making movies "faster and cheaper than their Hollywood counterparts."[11] The amount of time from filming to box office was shorter for small studios, so "it was easier for them to make films about current topics of interest . . . and to adjust more quickly their target audience": the American teenager.[12]

Many independent studios "populated their films with rubber-suited monsters, teenage delinquents, and mad scientists, representing a wholly different type of cinema—if not a different America—from the urbane sophistication of Hollywood productions."[13] The "cinemasochist" enjoys these types of movies, which many mainstream audiences would consider to be "bad" movies. Cinemasochists love these films "in spite of—or as often is the case, because [of the film's] technical limitations."[14] Robert Weiner points out that "the cinemasochist takes the same approach to film that Susan Sontag does in her *Notes on Camp*. . . . To paraphrase Oscar Wilde as she applies him to film studies: there are no good or bad movies; they are either charming or tedious."[15] *Mystery Science Theatre 3000 (MST3K)* may be credited for creating a broader cinemasochistic audience, as the cast of the show re-contextualized many "tedious" films into charming new works by using humorous running commentary, vocal riffing, and jokes. Additional humorous movie adaptation techniques before *MST3K* included "dialogue replacement and montage manipulation"; movies could be "completely transmuted through the construction of a new narrative."[16] Woody Allen's *What's Up, Tiger Lily?* (1966) for example, used vocal over-dubbing and rearranging of scenes to create a unique film, "wholly separate from the two existing [Japanese] films used to create it."[17] In 1973, the "Tiger Lily technique" of over-dubbing was also used by French Situationalists, who "redubbed the martial arts film *Crush* into *Can Dialectics Break Bricks*? replacing the plot with a variety of revolutionary messages and critiques of capitalism."[18] Meanwhile, "epitomized by characters such as Zacherley, Ghoulardi, Vampira and her early eighties reincarnation in the form of Elvira," the horror host provided audiences "with Z-grade features and glibly derisive commentary since the early 1950s."[19]

According to J. Hoberman, "it is possible for a movie to succeed because it has failed."[20] Hoberman focuses on the "supremely bad movie—[the] anti-masterpiece—[that] projects a stupidity that's fully as awesome as genius."[21] Certain films are valued not because they "fail on some level, but because they fail on every level, becoming a type of anti-cinema as rare and as valuable as a cinematic masterpiece."[22] Additionally, cinemasochism is related to empathy. Hoberman states, "to appreciate the humor and charm of one of the world's worst movies requires . . . a certain sympathy for and empathy with the hapless participants—not to mention a sense of irony about the very processes of cinematic illusion."[23]

The cult following of *The Rocky Horror Picture Show* (1975), for example, is early (and ongoing) evidence of how a large group of people can appreciate a film "that was critically and commercially unsuccessful upon its release, [and] who willfully 'subjected' themselves to it with a fetishistic fervor."[24] The "call-and-response audience participation" that has become a part of the *Rocky Horror* cultural phenomenon was "not intended by the filmmakers and wholly created by the fans themselves."[25] Jonathan Rosenbaum posits that "midnight movies [like *Rocky Horror* were] the most social form of film-going—even more than most home viewing."[26] Most importantly, though, nearly all of these precursors to sweded cinema chide from "a position of celebration rather than derision."[27] Following Rosenbaum, Jeffery Sconce recognizes that cinemasochists, rather than having "bad taste," instead possess sophisticated "cinematic knowledge" and have a "very refined and specific type of taste."[28] A cinemasochist knows more about cinema than a typical film fan and "chooses to watch such films as an act of rebellion against the mainstream assumption that such films are intrinsically bad."[29]

In a 1991 dialogue between Rosenbaum and Hoberman, Rosenbaum states that, "[t]he [movie] cults which coalesced during the early sixties were already dissenting from the popular ritual, which in this case was television."[30] Hoberman meanwhile wonders "whether [cinemasochistic] movies shouldn't be regarded, at least in part, as a phenomenon of economic depression, [and that] maybe what we're seeing is what remains of a dying industry—relocating itself where it can in relatively low-cost ventures."[31] Rosenbaum concludes, stating:

> If the mainstream has broadened to include more alternatives, it's in order to eliminate everything that exists outside of it. Midnight movies were basically a grass-roots, word-of-mouth phenomenon. What word-of-mouth means now is hearing from a friend at work about whatever big commercial blockbuster was being hyped on *Entertainment Tonight*. . . . And the glory of midnight movies is that they weren't advertised! Basically, they were created as media events by the audience. . . . *With the audience left to itself, new kinds of communal responses become possible—even if spectators are no longer in the same place.*[32]

Sweded videos similarly rebel from the popular ritual of passive movie watching. Thus, they might also be—at least in part—phenomena of economic depression, which invite community involvement and response. The major conflict in the film *Be Kind Rewind*, for example, revolves around evolving technologies (the popular turn from VHS to DVD) and the economic depression of the neighborhood of Passaic, New Jersey, where the film takes place. Sweded movies, which began popping up online, en masse, following the release of *Be Kind Rewind*, often reflect the community spirit and economic values portrayed in the movie. Additionally, aside from a few sweded movies that have received millions of hits on YouTube, most of these movies become "events" not through advertising or water cooler talk, but through social networking and email (our new word of mouth), and through the audience's voluntary decision to "subject themselves" to a (cinemasochistic) sweded movie: to search out, watch, and comment on the movie, and then possibly swede their own movie.

BE KIND REWIND: HOLLYWOOD DOES CINEMASOCHISM

In Michel Gondry's movie *Be Kind Rewind*, a VHS rental store is struggling to stay open, due to the competition of a DVD rental store that opens nearby. The socially inept friend (Jerry, played by Jack Black) of video store clerk, Mike (played by Mos Def) becomes physically magnetized, and accidentally erases every VHS tape in the store's stock. To keep the VHS rental store running, Mike and Jerry reshoot dozens of movies very quickly, with their own low-quality camera, no budget, and the support of a few creative, movie-loving friends. Their first remake is of *Ghostbusters*. When Mike realizes they have less than three hours to remake the whole film for a demanding customer, he shifts into high gear, telling Jerry, "I'm Bill Murray, you're everybody else. . . . She doesn't know what the movie is supposed to look like!" Mike gestures toward the video cover, "The only thing that she knows is what's on this box. She's never seen it before. If we stay 10 feet away from the camera she's not gonna recognize us. We come up with some special effects, we do it ourselves!"

Mike and Jerry thus dress up in aluminum foil suits and use Christmas garlands attached to fishing poles as the "beams" they shoot at imaginary ghosts in their public library. They recreate a night scene during the day by using the negative function on their camera and taping photocopies of their own faces to their heads. Housecats become demons jumping out of refrigerators, and their amicable mechanic friend Wilson plays all of the crucial female roles. After quickly planning and shooting 20 minutes of footage, Mike runs back to the store, putting the final touches on their version of *Ghostbusters*. He adds a voice-over of credits, quickly reading from the back of the movie box: "The end. Starring Bill Murray.

And other actors. Written by Dan Aykroyd. Directed by Ivan Reitman. Ghostbusters."[33]

Mike and Jerry's *Ghostbusters* reaches more than its intended audience of one. The next day, five young thug-like men enter the store holding the *Ghostbusters* remake and demand to know which other movies Mike and Jerry have made. To Mike's chagrin, Jerry tells the men "the whole store." (Really, the only other film they have made at this point in the movie is *Rush Hour 2*.) The young men pick out two movies they want to see: *Robocop* and *The Lion King*. To explain why the store needs a $20 deposit and 24 hours before they can rent these movies out, Jerry states that the movies are "custom made," and "Sweded." When the customer presses him about why they are called "Sweded" movies, Jerry responds that they are "a very rare type of video" and loosely connects this to Sweden being a "far away, expensive country," though it remains clear to the customers that the movies Mike and Jerry are making are not imported from Sweden, or anywhere else.[34]

Practices of producing low-budget versions of popular movies existed long before it was labeled "sweding" in *Be Kind Rewind*. For example, a shot-by-shot fan remake of *Raiders of the Lost Ark* (1981), which took seven years to complete, "premiered at the Alamo Drafthouse cinema on May 31st, 2003."[35] This type of re-making, sans the technology, is arguably as old as storytelling itself. The difference between sweded cinema and re-enacting *The Lord of the Rings* trilogy in your living room, however, involves not just a video camera, but also a set of (often loosely followed) rules, generated by the marketing and promotion of *Be Kind Rewind*: "On December 22nd, 2007, the BeKindMovie YouTube channel uploaded a video titled 'How to Swede' . . . with clips from the [upcoming] film, accompanied by commentary about how to produce a sweded film."[36] Two days after *Be Kind Rewind*'s release, the blog "Sweded Cinema" created a comprehensive list of rules for creating sweded videos:

1. Must be based on an already produced film
2. Range 2–8 minutes in length
3. Must not contain computer-generated graphics
4. Based on films less than 35 years old
5. Special effects must be limited to camera tricks and arts 'n crafts
6. Sound effects created by human means
7. Hilarious[37]

Sweding techniques are also present in some longer, collaborative, online works. The somewhat-sweded movie *Star Wars Uncut,* for example, is a remake of *Star Wars Episode IV: A New Hope* (1977). In 2009, Casey Pugh, Annelise Pruitt, Chad Pugh, and Jamie Wilkinson crowdsourced online, asking fans to sign up on their website to recreate 15-second scenes from the film. The 15-second scenes were then spliced together to remake the whole film. While a number of scenes for this project were created by following the rules of sweding, however, other scenes included animation and other sweding faux pas.

While *Be Kind Rewind* was a Hollywood endeavor, it was not a box office success, and the sweded movies it inspired do not incorporate Hollywood's aesthetic conventions, but rather parody these aesthetics. Much like when the Portapak (the first consumer-grade video camera) was released, sweders take advantage of newer and cheaper video making and sharing technologies, bringing the DIY, rough and tumble values of sweding into their homes and neighborhoods. They then often let their sweded movies loose online. Sweders take their knowledge (or lack thereof) of films and filmmaking, and their camera skills—ranging from amateur home video makers to the college educated and/or professionally trained—and *intentionally* create "bad" versions of "good" movies, with a very specific audience in mind: themselves, selected family and friends, and other cinemasochists with internet access.

RE-REWIND: ECHOES OF THE PORTAPAK IN SWEDED CINEMA

Sony first marketed portable consumer video equipment in the United States in 1965. According to Deirdre Boyle:

> Tripods, with their fixed viewpoints, were out; hand-held fluidity was in. Video's unique ability to capitalize on the moment with instant playback and real-time monitoring of events also suited the era's emphasis on "process, not product." Process art, earth art, conceptual art, and performance art all shared a deemphasis on the final work and an emphasis on how it came to be. The absence of electronic editing equipment which discouraged shaping a tape into a finished "product" further encouraged the development of a "process" video aesthetic.[38]

While critics of the Portapak faulted the new "underground" video's lack of technical quality, they also "praised it for carrying an immediacy rare in Establishment TV."[39] French New Wave filmmakers in the early 1960s had created a demand in Hollywood for "the grainy quality of cinema vérité, jump-cuts, and hand-held camera shots," rather than "glossy production" value.[40] Like their vérité predecessors, underground Portapak video pioneers "were inventing a new style, and they expected to dazzle the networks with their radical approach and insider's ability to get stories unavailable to commercial television."[41] The underground video making of the late 1960s became an aboveground media phenomenon in the 1970s. Yet, "when federal rules mandated local origination programming and public access channels for most cable systems, cable seemed to promise a new, Utopian era of democratic information, functioning as a decentralized alternative to the commercially-driven broadcast medium."[42]

YouTube and cheap digital video cameras ushered in a similar Utopian era of democratic information, this time breaking from both Hollywood and cable television aesthetics. What constitutes "information" on YouTube, however, is more nebulous. Information might be the video itself, regardless of its content, for instance. Community access groups of the 1970s learned that "once the novelty of exploring video equipment wore off, many community members had little interest in becoming video producers . . . [and] few had the time to develop the skills required to become producers of documentaries for broadcast."[43] By contrast, YouTube is available to many people who have access to and experience with home video technology. Yet, YouTube lacks the pressure to produce popular video for large *television* audiences. YouTube, like the Portapak, originally boasted its potential to "democratize" television. At the same time, all YouTube asked its users to do was "broadcast yourself."

The Portapak's "gritty, black-and-white tapes were generally edited in the camera, since editing was as yet a primitive matter of cut-and-paste or else a maddeningly imprecise back space method of cuing scenes for 'crash' edits."[44] The technological limitations of the video equipment dictated the style of the videos that were produced. Portapak "video pioneers of necessity were adept at making a virtue of their limitations."[45] This sentiment can also be found in sweded videos online, just with different limitations. The video equipment that many sweders use is of a much higher quality than the Portapak. Even cellphone videos—the current low standard of digital video—can be easily edited and enhanced. The limitations for sweders (as evident in the rules listed above) are primarily temporal, financial, and self-imposed. Rather than being limited by technology, sweders impose upon themselves a rather arbitrary short time limit, a promise to not include special effects or computer generated graphics, and an understanding that anything used in the sweded video should be inexpensive and/or already at hand—including the performers. Additionally, while early portable video "was not of broadcast quality," "ideal as an archival medium," or "practical for distribution,"[46] part of the reason for making sweded videos is both to broadcast and archive them.

An additional similarity between early Portapak filmmakers and present-day sweders is the sense of community established during the process of video-making. The Challenge for Change participatory video project, for example, was created by the National Film Board of Canada in 1967 to help combat poverty and initiate social change. The project put video cameras into the hands of socially underrepresented populations, allowing these community members to tell their own stories through video. Less concerned with the "quality" of the video produced, Challenge for Change sought to inspire community dialogue and social change in response to the issues brought up in and by the videos. According to Brian Rusted, "to view [Challenge for Change] community users as naïve participants in a cargo cult is to dismiss the complex, cultural sensory engagements that produce feelings of communitas. Embedded in the narrative and editing structures are turning-point moments . . . that produce various community transformations as the process unfolds."[47] The communitas Rusted refers to has to do with participants' changing attitudes toward local social and cultural issues. The communitas evoked by sweding, however, includes both nostalgia for, and a parodic attitude toward the illusion of big-budget Hollywood films. Yet, in both cases, process takes precedence over product. Rusted points out that "Portapaks did contribute to new ways of seeing, as is conveyed in the voice-over of [the video] VTR St-Jacques: 'You know, I walk around here every day and I pass by things without even noticing them and when I look through the camera I really see.'"[48] Similarly, sweded videos offer their audiences new ways of seeing Hollywood movies—through the creative vision and adaptation of other movie watchers. Sweded movies also often unabashedly call attention to their kitschy, DIY aesthetic. They are Brechtian in this way, distancing audiences by letting the footlights show, as Brecht might say; always calling attention to their own constructedness, and by doing so, attempting to eliminate any possibility of Hollywood illusion. Sweded movies inherently challenge illusionism by constantly reminding the viewer how *not real* they are.

According to Rusted, "Despite the frequent recognition that the video product should not overshadow the video process, the desire to have tapes reach beyond the local, closed-circuit setting shortened the product life of the Portapak."[49] The ideal audience for sweded videos can range from the video makers only, to a potentially global audience. Internet video-sharing sites make any of these audiences a possibility for sweders. Finally, regarding the Challenge for Change project, and early portable video, Rusted states: "Each successive project stands in for those prior performances of the process. They are not representations of bodies in a process. The making and the use of the videos are bodily re-enactments of the process. As technological and material practices, they are multi-sensory performances of the process of social change. The 'films per se may be worthless' but the process they perform is not."[50] This statement echoes how Connerton interweaves inscribing and incorporating practices, and could apply just as well to sweded videos. Perhaps sweded films, with their low production value, cheesy performances, and trashy sets and costumes are economically worthless when compared to Hollywood norms. However, the processes of learning and creation, and how sweders critique Hollywood culture using Hollywood texts, are similarly "multi-sensory performances of the process of social change."[51]

THE NEVERENDING STORY (SWEDED)

Sweding is kind of like playing at movie making. Imagine—if you will—kids who throw a party with stuffed animals or dolls in lieu of real guests; they are imitating the actions of their predecessors with what they have seen and what is at hand. Sweders do a similar thing (imitation using what is at hand), and add video technology. Sweding is often done by adults, so the imitation also often comes with a knowing wink at the audience. The sweded video says "I know I'm a bad video," and simultaneously asserts, "I know you're watching precisely because you know I'm going to be a bad video—one that you might really enjoy!" The sweded video calls its enthusiastic viewers out as what they are: cinemasochists.

The sweded version of *The Neverending Story* was one of the first sweded videos that my internal cinemasochist fell in love with. Created by Brandon Todd and Brian Simpson over the course of four weekends, the video cost 25 dollars to make.[52] For those who have not seen or don't remember the original version, the following description may not be amusing. However, for those who love the movie like I do, I'll list some of the impressive ways that these sweders adapted and condensed the story and characters, and created fun, cheesy special effects:

- The large storybook that Bastian reads throughout most of the movie has a large pretzel taped to the front of it, rather than the original metal, snake-like insignia.
- The Rockbiter munches on a packet of Pop Rocks, and is made out of brown paper bags and a baseball mitt. He is made to look enormous through creative camera placement and framing, and the use of an extreme low-angle shot.
- The Ivory Tower is represented by a bottle of Ivory dish soap.
- Artec is played by a horse-head on a stick, and dies not by sinking into *quicksand*, but by "sinking" (i.e., being dragged) through a black garbage bag with a hole cut into it.
- An ET doll with a shell on its back plays Moria, the giant, melancholy turtle.
- A toy Skeletor is used in place of the skeleton that Atreyu finds in the sand.
- An adorable puppy plays Falkor.
- Another adorable puppy plays the wolf—a character that *gave me nightmares* as a child.
- When Bastian calls out the Childlike Empress's name, the name is at least ten syllables long, and is hilarious in its extreme, intentional unintelligibility.

- Many different camera angles and visual tricks are used to give the viewer the impression that certain elements are much farther away, closer, larger, or smaller than they really are.
- All of the music and sound effects are created using peoples' voices.
- During the theme song, several voices tentatively sing the verse, and some of the words are unintelligible. When they get to the chorus, however, more voices chime in and they all confidently sing the catchiest part of the song—"The Neverending Stooo-ory! Oh-oh-oh, oh-oh-oh, oh-oh-oh!"[53]

This video is amusing to me for the above reasons, and then some. It is silly, playful, and fun. The sweders also send up what I consider to be some of the best and most memorable scenes in the movie, with a wink and a nod toward the informed viewer who has seen *The Neverending Story*. *The Neverending Story* was released in 1984 (when I was just a kid), and I couldn't get enough of it. The sweded version helps me remember what I loved so much about the original movie, while showing the adult me how ridiculous the movie is and *always has been*. This sweded version of *The Neverending Story* makes me nostalgic for my childhood. Its existence gives me the impression that others are similarly nostalgic for theirs. At the same time, the sweded version's cheesy performances and cheap but creative aesthetic pokes fun at all of the special effects and magical creatures that won my heart and baffled my mind as a child. Thus, rather than take a melancholy spin, my nostalgia makes me want to share in the fun, creativity, and laughter.

SHARING SWEDED CINEMA—OR—TRYING TO SPREAD THE FUN

> Hi Michael!
> Truthiness, songification, and sweding are of course on my list of words that couldn't possibly be more awesome. :) And then there's this: http://www.youtube.com/watch?v=dOwNwsxaW5k&feature=related[54]

WILLY WONKA AND THE CHOCOLATE FACTORY (SWEDED)

The above link leads to a dizzying, two-minute sweded version of *Willy Wonka and the Chocolate Factory*, in which one man plays almost all of the characters. The video begins with the man in a supermarket, wearing a stripy shirt and wig, holding a Wonka Bar and singing to us about how delicious it is. We proceed through a "Wonkomania" newscast, and several seconds later, we see Charlie in his bright red sweater, holding a Wonka Bar. Charlie opens the bar, finds the golden ticket, and sings and dances his way down the street. We are swiftly transported to the Chocolate Factory. Colorful umbrellas, scarves, and balloons line the walls of someone's living room, creating a kitschy yet magical aesthetic. Our Willy Wonka sings and dances down the stairs of his Chocolate Kingdom. We cut to Augustus Gloop, who is drinking out of the "chocolate river," i.e., a bathtub filled with brown, watery, liquid. Augustus falls in and splashes around in the water. After a few seconds of this we hear a woman—assumedly the one holding the camera—say "Go under now!" Gloop dunks his head hesitantly into the unidentifiable liquid. Next, Veruca Salt throws her temper tantrum, demanding a golden egg. The chute that Veruca falls down is made out of a cardboard box and some aluminum foil. She steps into the box, and an Oompa Loompa helps pull the box up the length of her body and over her head, while he points to the words "Bad Egg." Moments later, an anonymous person (or mannequin) plays Charlie (we recognize Charlie only by his red sweater), never facing the camera. Wonka ducks behind the anonymous person to fill in Charlie's lines, and jumps back out to say his own. The movie concludes with a miniature-scale foil elevator breaking through the roof of a cardboard building. Charlie and Willie Wonka fly over the city in the elevator, which is held up by a highly visible string, and very reminiscent of the UFOs in Ed Wood Jr.'s infamous *Plan 9 from Outer Space* (regarded by some as the worst movie of all time).[55] All of this happens in exactly two minutes.

Perhaps I am drawn to this version of *Willy Wonka and the Chocolate Factory* because it is another movie I loved as a child. Like the sweded version of *The Neverending Story*, this video brings up a mix of childhood nostalgia and adult playfulness for me. The singing, dancing, stuffed animals, and ridiculous props remind me of "playing pretend" as a child. Sometimes this pretend play took a form similar to sweding, sans the video camera. My brothers and I would reenact scenes from our favorite movies and television shows, using toys as props and relying on ourselves to play *all* of the parts. Again, the nostalgia I get from watching this video also simultaneously plants me squarely in the present, and reminds me that it is okay to be silly—ridiculous even—as an adult. It is okay to have fun.

SPREADING THE FUN #FAIL —OR— SWEDING *DIRTY HARRY*: INSPIRATION

Hi Lynz,
First, the link: Methinks some people have too much time on their hands. :) And I have no idea what they're doing, anyway. Now, if you

could send me a sweded version of, say, "Dirty Harry," I'd probably eat that up with a big spoon.[56] ~ M

CHALLENGE ACCEPTED!

In September 2012, I scoured the internet for a sweded version of *Dirty Harry* that I could forward to Michael. I wanted to spread the joy of sweding, but forwarding my favorite sweded movies had clearly not worked. I found only one record of a sweded version of *Dirty Harry,* but its creator had taken it down. Hours of YouTube searches produced no results, beyond a number of adaptations of the scene in which Dirty Harry asks, "Do you feel lucky? Well, do ya, *punk*?" I was not feeling so lucky.

Mental light bulb! I would swede *Dirty Harry*! Of course! I had sweding experience, as I had sweded versions of *Rush Hour 2, Labyrinth,* and *The Birds* with some friends in early 2008. I had creativity, drive, a couple ideas, and a few good friends who agreed to help. One slight catch: I had never seen *Dirty Harry*.

SWEDING *DIRTY HARRY*: HESITATION

I watched *Dirty Harry* once in October 2012, and made numerous plans to swede the movie. These plans fell through, month after month. A year later, when I felt more than ready to swede this beast, I realized that I didn't own or even have convenient access to a video camera. Thus, it was not until late 2013 that I made definite plans to swede *Dirty Harry*. No backing out this time. I was a little nervous and a little excited. My audience would be me, my friends, and possibly anonymous internet users (other cinemasochists who like *Dirty Harry,* or like sweded videos). This video would also be a gift for Michael, and an homage and sendup of *Dirty Harry*. I wanted the video to be all wrong in all of the right ways. I wanted it to be hilarious. I wanted to have fun making it. I imagined it would be personally embarrassing and awkwardly fulfilling. I imagined that *everyone* would want to play the Scorpio Killer—I know I did. But I'd be too busy directing. Directing a sweded movie as part of this study would give me valuable insight into the process of sweding that I would be unable to get just by watching sweded videos or reading about the phenomenon. To really try to understand sweding, as a process-based creative form, my research had to include an enactment of sweding.

MAKING SPACE, TAKING LIBERTIES

To revisit Deb Margolin's theories about parody, which I discussed in chapter 1:

> [P]arody is the direct result of an attempt to make room for oneself within an airtight, closed, or exclusive social, cultural, or theatrical construct. A kind of aria of the poor. It is an inherently ridiculous act, like a woman in a housedress crashing a fancy party. That's why, although not all parody is funny, parody is considered to be a subset of comedy. Parody is a desperate act of love, it does not exist without some form of love, of passion, of desire. There is no point in the parody of something with which one is not actively and passionately engaged. Parody is the brashest and most heart-rending voice of the outsider looking in. . . . Parody is an act of burglary by an inexperienced and weird burglar. The outsider status of the parodist sometimes lends parody an angry or sarcastic edge, but parody is almost always an act of aspiration. It is the clumsy, refreshing voice of the uninvited we hear in a parodical presentation. Parody, then, has immediate and implicit political signification, because the site of its humor is the gap between actor and character—what the character is that the actor is not. Parody, by this definition, is evoked by a cultural environment in which the purveyor is either not wanted, not needed, or both.[57]

Many sweded movies offer at least a hint of tongue-in-cheek creativity. Many are over-the-top, and obviously parodic, but in the most loving way. A sweded movie is an ode in Margolin's "aria of the poor," a labor of love. Regarding her own performances as Hamlet, Margolin states, "the script didn't need my liberties, but it got them, because I needed them to make room for myself, to paint my image on the larger canvas of this magnificent work."[58] Similarly, *Dirty Harry* didn't need the liberties that we were about to impose upon it, but the sweding cast I pulled together needed these liberties. The self-imposed temporal and financial limitations of sweding, along with a group of performers with a variety of relations to *Dirty Harry* (one performer watched the movie for the tenth time the morning we sweded it, and another had never seen it), necessitated some space. Before beginning, we all knew that our adaptation of *Dirty Harry* would include so-called mistakes, ad-libs, and other performance excesses. For my part, as director and cinematographer, the camerawork might have only a vague resemblance to the original movie. Yet, as sweders, we needed to make space for ourselves in the cultural phenomenon of *Dirty Harry*. We each brought our voice and interpretation, including performers with a lack of *Dirty Harry* knowledge, but an interest in participating in the project. We combined our visions and intentions to create *our* "Dirty Harry." We had my condensed shooting script, camerawork, and editing; Ariel's and John's cheesy performances (or parodies) of Clint Eastwood's and Andy Robinson's original performances of Dirty Harry and the Scorpio Killer; Lauren's and Mike's willingness to wear goofy costumes, take artistic direction, improvise, and go with the flow; and the many ideas that came up during our process of shooting the movie. All of these performances, lifted from traditional moviemaking conventions and adapted for sweding, manifested in a fun day (and night) with friends, a sense of accomplishment and pride for each of us, and our final product, "Dirty Harry—SWEDED."

Margolin states, "perhaps, at its best, parody can render its object a palimpsest of meanings, and deepen the viewer's relationship with that object."[59] I think that sweding can't help but be parodic, in Margolin's sense. I now think about *Dirty Harry* in a more complex, fake blood, real sweat, and laughter to tears kind of way. I imagine other "Dirty Harry—SWEDED" viewers will have a new take on *Dirty Harry* as well.

THE MOVIE, THE LEGEND, THE STORY

"Lean and loping, with hides like an old boot"; This is what action movies felt like, before the Hollywood Blockbuster era, according to Tom Shone. Shone states, "In the seventies, the job of action director was essentially a specialty act, a renegade career path, the province of lone wolfs like Walter Hill and Don Siegel—tough leathery types who peeled off from the Hollywood pack to pay their silent debt to Sam Peckinpah and Howard Hawkes with movies that were set in the city—*The Taking of Pelham One Two Three, The Driver, Dirty Harry*—but which felt like Westerns."[60] Then in the 1980s, "everyone joined in [and] action movie-making became a loud raucous party."[61] The action movie got a complete makeover, "losing its air of civic sweat and moral unease, to make way for a brasher, bright air of hard-edged modernity."[62] *Dirty Harry* made way for blockbusters like *Die Hard.* Blockbusters like *Die Hard* eventually made way for sweded versions of themselves, born of homage, camp aesthetics, love, and cinemasochistic performers who wanted to remake their favorite movies.

Candice Hopkins posits, "[i]n art, since the dawn of mechanical reproduction, the copy is understood as subversive: Its very presence (particularly if there is potential for infinite replication) challenges the authority of the original."[63] However, sweding is less like copying and more like storytelling. Hopkins explains how replication in storytelling (unlike copying) "is positive and necessary," stating that "[i]t is through change that stories . . . are kept alive and remain relevant. In the practice of storytelling, there is no desire for originality, as stories that are told and retold over time are not individual but communal: they are made by, and belong to, many."[64] Similarly, regarding storytelling, Trinh Minh-ha states that "[i]n this chain and continuum, I am but one link. The story is not me, neither me nor mine. It does not really belong to me, and while I feel greatly responsible for it, I also enjoy the irresponsibility of the pleasure obtained through the process of transferring. No repetition can ever be identical, but my story carries with it their stories, their history, and our story repeats itself endlessly."[65]

Meanwhile, according to Henry Jenkins, our spectator culture is giving way to a more participatory culture. The average citizen now has the control to seize multiple media to tell any story in various ways. Jenkins connects current digital media culture to the storytelling traditions of thousands of years ago (the same oral cultures that Hopkins alludes to), a time when the stories of various communities belonged to the people who told and listened to them. In a YouTube video about Hollywood and participatory culture, for example, Jenkins states, "Those images now belong to major media companies," as he stands in Times Square in front of a large screen playing Disney's version of *Cinderella*. Yet, in the digital age, Jenkins posits that people are reasserting their rights to stories, taking the stories back without copyright permissions. Jenkins states that we are "innovating, experimenting, recontextualizing, [and] responding to" these images in new ways.[66] Jenkins speaks fluidly about stories and images, making no distinction between the two.

Sweders are not necessarily "taking back" stories and/or images, as much as they are staking claim to their right and their ability to *tell stories* through processes of performance, parody, and video adaptation. The stories that sweded movies tell all originate from Hollywood movies, yet the process-over-product values of sweding are so removed from Hollywood aesthetics that most sweded movies fly under US and (YouTube's Content ID) copyright radar. Meanwhile, sweded movies retell Hollywood's stories, and tell the story of Hollywood, through a loving but critical lens. By sweding *Dirty Harry*, for example, we are specifically telling the story of Dirty Harry. We are also propagating the more general crime story, the western story, and the story of the no-nonsense vigilante hero who is the only one with the guts to do whatever needs to be done. On the other hand, when we swede *Dirty Harry*, we have the option of including or cutting whatever we choose. Eastwood's Dirty Harry, for example (on whom the lessons of the Civil Rights Movement, in general, seem to be lost), can be adapted to be more likeable for present-day audiences. We can cut his racist, homophobic, and sexist remarks. We can subvert Dirty Harry's signature phallic Magnum .44 by giving him a tiny purple squirt gun to hold each time he tells us about his "44 Magnum, the most powerful handgun on earth." We can reshape Dirty Harry's 1971 mindset, which today comes off as that of an out-of-touch sociopath, to make him more sympathetic (or at the very least, intentionally funny) to contemporary viewers. We can re-script *Dirty Harry*, the scriptive thing.

My merry gang of sweders and I thus set out to swede *Dirty Harry* with loving hearts, critical eyes, and playful attitudes. The story of *Dirty Harry*, as Minh-ha would say, "is not me, neither me nor mine. It does not really belong to me, and while I [felt] greatly responsible for it, I also enjoy[ed] the irresponsibility of the pleasure obtained through the process of transferring."[67]

SWEDING *DIRTY HARRY*: ON SET

I inform my collaborators that the sweding will commence at 4:30 pm. The day before the swede, I borrow a video camera, watch *Dirty Harry* (for the second time ever), and find, gather, and borrow any props and costumes I imagine we'll need. The morning of the swede, I put together a six-page shooting script, organized into day and night shots, and by the characters involved in each shot, and I and print several copies. I also create a school bus on my front porch, using a wooden table with an orange travel towel taped to the front of it, 5 chairs, stuffed animal "students," and a steering wheel made from a paper plate. Black electrical tape lines the orange towel, creating a homely front grille on the bus. I forget to make headlights. It's a pathetic excuse for a school bus, really. C'est la vie. I have no doubt that my collaborators will be able to *create* the necessary bus through their performances, nonetheless.

Three of the four performers show up between 4:30 and 5. Dirty Harry, played by Ariel Gratch, shows up first, already in costume, and probably already sweating. He's wearing at least three layers of clothing (as shown in figure 5.1) and we are in Baton Rouge, where it is 90 degrees outside and sunny, with 44 percent humidity. Ariel's had a long day at work, and his generally cheerful voice is naturally beginning to sound like the raspy and ornery Clint Eastwood.

The Scorpio Killer, played by John LeBret, brings a bag of costume options and some extra ketchup, at my request, in case we need fake blood. He starts making Scorpio's peace sign belt buckle out of aluminum foil, telling me that he watched *Dirty Harry* again that morning. John's hair is windswept, appropriately Scorpio-tousled. Lauren Leist brings her swimsuit, even though that part of the filming will be done at *her* apartment complex; all I asked her to do for the video was to play "the pretty woman who gets shot while swimming." Lauren, glancing at my coffee table, which is covered in props, scripts, stuffed animals, wigs, and costumes, laughs and admits that she has no idea what we're doing. I ask if she knows what sweding is. "No," she responds.

"Okay," I say, "We're basically remaking *Dirty Harry* today, with all of this stuff. An eight-minute version. Have you ever seen *Dirty Harry*?" I ask her.

"No," Lauren responds, with a hesitant smile.

"Perfect," I say. I hand her a script.[68]

Our final player, Mike Rold, will join us later that evening. We begin with who we have. At 5 pm, after everyone has looked over the script, we

Figure 5.1. First shootout scene of "Dirty Harry—SWEDED." Dirty Harry played by Ariel Gratch.
***Source*: Image courtesy of the author.**

start shooting. Outside first, daytime shots that involve only Dirty Harry, Scorpio, and voiceovers. Lauren vocally makes the gunshot noises for our first shoot-out scene, and John does the voiceover for the first punk, who is played by a small, white, stuffed bunny, as shown in figure 5.2.

SWEDING *DIRTY HARRY*: DAYLIGHT FADING

Despite the stifling heat, everyone is in great spirits and having a good time. Our first real technical snafu occurs within the first 15 minutes of shooting. Dirty Harry tells his partner Gonzales, played by a stuffed monkey wearing a foil police badge, to "go check on the mother," after they discover a dead body on the lawn across the street from my house. Dirty Harry's direction, at this point, was to throw the monkey out of the shot, which he did. Gonzales, however, landed in a nearby tree; a priceless image that, while unfaithful to the movie, I had to film. I anticipated that I would want to include this in our final cut (and I did). Glorious excess.

Lauren, meanwhile, filled in sound effects, voiceovers, and minor characters whenever needed. In one hour, she played the Mayor (wearing my suit jacket), a judge (wearing Ariel's graduation robe), a dead body, and the voice of the man who beats Scorpio up for $200. Lauren's direction for this role was to "try to sound like an older black man . . . but without sounding racist. Like, think of Robert Downey Jr. in the movie *Tropic Thunder*." I paused, realizing how difficult it is to give non-racist

Figure 5.2. "Dirty Harry—SWEDED," the injured "punk."
***Source*: Image courtesy of the author.**

directions for an originally racist scene. The scene includes plot points I want to keep, and language I want to cut. I'm squeamish. "That's still kind of racist," I confirm. "Just sound old and raspy. And very calm. Not necessarily black. Just old. What? Okay . . . Just read the lines." This marked my first directorial decision to cut some of the racism in the original *Dirty Harry* out of our version. Further, it seems I was not alone in terms of being uncomfortable with the content of this particular scene (among others):

> Andrew Robinson [who played the Scorpio Killer] is a pacifist who despises guns. In the early days of principal photography, Robinson would flinch violently every time he fired. Director Don Siegel was forced to shut down production for a time and sent Robinson to a school to learn to fire a gun convincingly. However, he still blinks noticeably when he shoots. Robinson was also squeamish about filming the scene where he verbally and physically abuses several schoolchildren, and the scene where he racially insults the man he pays to beat him up.[69]

SWEDING *DIRTY HARRY*: AT THE DOCKS

After finishing as many daytime shots as we could at my house, we headed out for some destination shots. The Mississippi River, only blocks away, seemed the ideal spot to shoot the dock scene where Dirty Harry kills Scorpio. We drove up the river to an old dock Ariel suggested, only to discover that access to the dock had been torn down. We stood around for a few minutes, trying to think of another spot. Meanwhile, I took advantage of the daylight and our useless dock to get a couple shots we might be able to use for other parts of the movie. Indeed, both "useless" shots were used at the end of our final cut, after Dirty Harry kills Scorpio and walks off into the distance.

We decided that we could probably find a location near some water at the nearby Louisiana State University lakes. Indeed, we found a perfectly isolated, gorgeous dock there. Lauren was cast, again on the spot, in the role of "that kid who is fishing and gets held hostage," as I quickly explained to her.

"Do we have a fishing pole?" Ariel asked me as we parked the car.

Dammit. "No. I figured we could just find a stick or something," I responded, as if I'd planned this, rather than forgotten it. As we walk toward the dock, I spot a single fallen branch. Ariel and John bring it to over to our spot, laughing. Close up, it is not so much a branch as it is a tree limb. It's enormous. We work with what we have, sending Lauren up the dock in a new wig, with a gigantic fishing pole, as seen in figure 5.3.

Our location, along with the sunset hour we've reached, allows for some amazing takes of Dirty Harry's final monologue and Scorpio's death scene. Aware of time (and sunlight), I try to get through the dock shots quickly. Because of how beautiful the location is, I want these shots, in particular, to at least *look* perfect. Ariel, possibly giddy from the heat, is struggling to say his line, "Being this is a .44 Magnum, the most powerful handgun on earth." Or rather, he is struggling to say this line and glance

Figure 5.3. Scorpio (played by John LeBret), as he takes his final hostage—a kid fishing on a dock, using a large tree limb (played by Lauren Leist).
***Source*: Image courtesy of the author.**

at his cocked purple squirt gun without laughing. We do multiple takes of this shot, from Dirty Harry's point of view and from Scorpio's (as shown in figures 5.4 and 5.5). Later, as I'm researching the famous "Magnum .44 monologue" I learn that Ariel was not alone in his inability to perform the line as written:

> According to the original script, the phrase that Dirty Harry quotes during both the bank robbery and his final confrontation with Scorpio was not the actual quote for the movie, the actual quote in the script was, "Well? Was it five or was it six? Regulations say five . . . hammer down on an empty . . . only not all of us go by the book. What you have to do is think about it. I mean, this is a .44 Magnum and it'll turn your head into hash. Now, do you think I fired five or six? And if five, do I keep a live one under the hammer? It's all up to you. Are you feeling lucky, punk?"[70]

We still need to shoot the pool scene before the sun goes down, so we speed over to Lauren's apartment. Lauren, conveniently, has a balcony that overlooks her apartment complex's pool. The location is perfect for the pool scene *and* several shots I forgot to get while we were still at the lake. These include a large splash in the water to indicate that Scorpio has fallen in and the shot of Dirty Harry throwing his police badge out into the lake. Though it's a hot Louisiana evening, and, according to Lauren, there were hordes of people at the pool when she left at 4:30 pm, the pool is perfectly deserted. Lauren dons her swimsuit and heads down to dive and swim gracefully, and to pretend she gets shot in the pool—again, the only scene she knew she'd be in. We also use Lauren as a body double in

Figure 5.4. Dirty Harry's final monologue on the dock, from Scorpio's point of view.
***Source*: Image courtesy of the author.**

Figure 5.5. The Scorpio Killer, moments before his demise.
***Source*: Image courtesy of the author.**

this location: she cannonballs herself into the pool to create a huge splash that I will later use in Scorpio's death scene.

We finish the pool shots, meet up with Mike, and drive back to my place. There are a number of scenes we still have to shoot. Opting to shoot the outdoor scenes first, while it's still dusk, we find a patch of grass that is *slightly* better lit than others. The streetlights are on, and I try to shoot several scenes under one. It's much too dark. I tell myself, "I'll fix it in post." I simultaneously tell myself, "There is no 'fix it in post' in sweding!" I have no back-up plan.

We find a nearby building to use that has well-lit pillars. While shooting the scene where Dirty Harry and Scorpio first meet face-to-face, Ariel looks exhausted, impatient. He is tired, hot, and in pain. But now it's finally John's turn to shine on camera, and I want to give him that chance. We hurry through several shots of Scorpio, including the infamous turn-and-scream shot, after Dirty Harry stabs Scorpio in the leg. For this shot, John happily dons a homemade "ski mask" I created by cutting holes into a long pink winter hat, and he looks appropriately ridiculous. Meanwhile, I'm mentally cutting the outdoor night scenes we have not filmed yet and wondering if we can do without them. We will have to.

Ariel takes a much-needed break to cool down while we film the bus scenes on my porch with John and Mike. Mike puts on a homely pink dress and brown wig I pulled out of my closet and inquires politely about his character and motivation.

"You're a bus driver," I say. I am also spent, mentally and physically. Mike wants more.

"Can I be old? He calls me a hag, I think I'm old," Mike states.

"Yes, be old," I agree.

"What kind of bus driver am I?" Mike asks.

I laugh. "The kind that is driving a group of kids home and gets hijacked by a serial killer." It's the best I can do, and Mike seems satisfied. We begin shooting the bus scenes, and Mike becomes a bizarre, jolly, elderly bus driver with an oddly affected southern accent, who seems to *really* enjoy driving. John's performances of the kids' songs on the bus are half-improvised, full of pep, and hilarious. Lauren and I fill in the voices of the crying and singing children from behind the camera. I realize at this point that I never told Mike about certain moviemaking protocols that I take for granted: Things like "Do not look directly into the camera unless I tell you to," "Don't smile when you're supposed to be scared," and "Please, Mike, for the last time, keep your script off screen!" Alas, these are *movie-making* protocols, and we are not making a movie; we are sweding a movie. These details, mistakes that would require an additional take while shooting a movie, are part of what will set our video apart as sweded, rather than just a poor remake. What we have is solid sweding gold.

SWEDING *DIRTY HARRY*: BUTTER KNIVES, PAYPHONES, AND OTHER EXCESSES

Back inside the house, Ariel is refreshed and ready to shoot the final scenes, including two scenes with the police chief and the phone booth scenes. Mike puts on a hat and black jacket, and borrows the badge Ariel has been using all day. Boom: Police Chief. In one scene with our police chief, Dirty Harry tapes a knife to his leg—the same knife with which he later stabs Scorpio. We use a butter knife for this scene, for the sake of hilarity. On the spot, I feed Mike a line I had decided to cut earlier in the day. As Dirty Harry uses scotch tape to bind the knife to his leg, the chief states, "It's disgusting that police officers have to know how to use a weapon like that." Meanwhile, Ariel is struggling with the scotch tape. He has wrapped the tape around his ankle a few times (I forgot to tell him he only needed a small piece), and he cannot get it to cut using the tape dispenser. Ariel ends up with a string of twisted tape about three feet long, all of which he wraps around his ankle before giving the tape dispenser back to Mike. We obviously don't need a second take.

My concept for the phone booth sequence had been stewing for a long time. I decided how we should stage these scenes the day I saw *Dirty Harry* for the first time. A full-size poster of a red telephone booth hangs on my living room wall. I wanted to use that poster, with a rotary dial phone next to it, as every phone booth Dirty Harry goes to. I would shoot from different angles, but it would obviously be the same silly, fake phone booth. In between these shots, I would splice in shots of Dirty

Harry running in random spots throughout town. At the last minute, Ariel decided to splash himself with water between each phone booth shot, so that Dirty Harry would appear to get increasingly sweaty (as seen in figure 5.6). Performer ideas, suggestions, and "mistakes" created some of the funniest moments of our *Dirty Harry*. And this process, of keeping mistakes and excesses for the sake of humor, might not be too different from some things that happened on set during the filming of the original *Dirty Harry*. For example, "When Harry finally meets Scorpio in Mount Davidson Park, Scorpio orders him to show his gun with his left hand. Harry pulls it from his holster and Scorpio ad-libs the line, 'My, that's a big one!' This line caused the crew to crack up and the scene had to be re-shot, but the line stayed."[71]

PERFECTLY IN JUST ONE TAKE

Creativity flourishes with limitations in any context. For example, "[f]or the iconic final shot when Dirty Harry tosses away his badge, Don Siegel was dismayed to discover that they had only brought one badge to the location shoot, so Eastwood had to throw it perfectly in just one take."[72] Unlike this pressure for perfection of product, however, technological limitations and the lowered expectations for a final product almost always take a back seat to the expectations of the process for a sweded movie. During the film shoot we expect to have fun, learning, laughing, *together* in space and time, while creating something we know will not

Figure 5.6. Dirty Harry's fifth phone booth scene, of six, showing his extreme "perspiration."
***Source*: Image courtesy of the author.**

bring us monetary success. The success here is in the process, which is paramount. The product is the strawman that I used to bring us all together, perhaps. But in the end, we all know that our product—at best—will be brilliant low art. This is what we celebrate during and after the process. We perform for our future cinemasochistic audience and ourselves.

As a method of digital adaptation and digital performance, sweding is descendent from earlier cinemasochistic forms. However, the riffing in sweding happens through self-imposed limitations. The excess, in a sense, is created by the improvisatory changes that come from clearly not having enough of something (money, time, people), rather than external vocal riffing (like *MST3K*), creative subtitling (as I discuss in chapter 4), or some change in the narrative. The excess in sweding comes from trying to stay true to the narrative, while knowing this is impossible. Excess in sweding is often by accident, by mistake. It's ad-lib. Meanwhile, the respected and/or big budget film is transformed into a short, funny, Z-grade homage. The bad movie is not made for Hollywood audiences, but instead for the participatory, cinemasochistic, already-a-fan audience. The sweded video, at its best, builds the spirit of "I want to do that!" in the audience. Indeed, after posting *Dirty Harry-SWEDED* to YouTube, I was asked by many people, "what's the next one going to be?"—a question that generally came with suggestions and an offer to help with the "next one." This is the community of creators and network of viewers for the sweded video: the knowing, cinemasochistic audience. Whether that audience knows the movie or the people doing the sweding (or both) is not necessarily relevant.

SWEDING *DIRTY HARRY*: FIXING IT IN POST

The morning after sweding *Dirty Harry*, I build the movie. I have 25 minutes of video and 82 shots. I realize now that sweding is as much about breaking (or perhaps stretching) the rules as it is about following them. After about five hours of editing on my computer—even though I was probably *supposed to* edit and cut in-camera—I am down to ten minutes of video and some hard choices. Some of the chase scenes are oddly quiet; should I add asynchronous sound? Remembering how we used someone's cell phone ring to shoot the phone booth scenes the night before (nobody wanted to make a ringing noise), I decide to go with a minimal amount of added music. Do I cut more to fit the correct length? Do I insert *just one* scene transition I want to include between the opening credits and the first flash of Scorpio's gun? Again, this was something I was hoping to be able to shoot somehow, but we didn't have enough sunlight to pull it off. I add the transition and look at the rules again, feeling a little guilty.

"Must be based on an already produced film." Yes. "Range 2–8 minutes in length." My final cut falls outside of this range at 10 minutes, a bit of a stretch. "Must not contain computer-generated graphics." Check. "Based on films less than 35 years old." What?! Suddenly the list of rules seems absolutely stupid and arbitrary. *Dirty Harry* came out in 1971. The film is 42 years old. I am having my own Veruca Salt temper tantrum. *Willy Wonka and the Chocolate Factory* also came out in 1971, and the sweded version of that movie is *brilliant* (in my opinion), and has more than 360,000 hits on YouTube.[73] I decide that rules are made for breaking. "Special effects must be limited to camera tricks and arts 'n crafts." Aside from the one transition I added, we followed this rule. "Sound effects created by human means." Again, other than the bit of music I added and the telephone ring, we did this. We even took turns making the gunshot noises for the shootout scenes. "Hilarious." Absolutely.

I condense the whole of *Dirty Harry* down to a 10-minute sweded movie. It felt a bit like adapting a written novel into a one-act performance. With the novel, though, there is often more space for interpretation. The adapter doesn't always have to contend with past performances of the story. With video, we have to make space for ourselves, as Deb Margolin might say, for more voices and bodies beyond those in the original film. Because of this condensing, the final product may not make sense to someone who is unfamiliar with the original movie. However, the space we've made for ourselves should be apparent to anyone who has seen the original. Our excesses with *Dirty Harry*—the monkey in the tree, ad-libs, accidents, un-cut-able scotch tape, and most of Lauren's performances—are funny when considered in the context of the original movie. We bring something new to the work. The movie didn't need our liberties, but it got them. The sweded movie is thus a kind of inside joke for an inside audience, including those who are familiar with (and like) the film, the group who makes the video, and the friends and family members with whom this group wants to share their video.

SWEDING: COMMUNITY, NETWORKS, AND TECHNO-PLAY

Bianca Stigter states:

> On the web the difference between creators and users, between producers and consumers, between artists and audiences fades, but not in such a degree that those borders can be discarded. But the means to create art have been democratized. Maybe film is going to look more and more like music in this point of view, where at home people no longer just listen to it. Music is being played, criticized, performed. Maybe film scenarios one day will become something like written music.[74]

Sweding is a potentially larger and more time-consuming enterprise than creatively subtitling or reenacting, which I discuss in chapters 2 through 4. Rather than working with video and text, or short video and bodies, sweding projects potentially require more work and have more limitations. What is at stake for sweders, however, is far less fleeting than other forms of digital video adaptation. Sweders add voices, visions, and bodies to the legacy of whatever movie they've chosen. Yet, sweded movies are still an art form that "at home people" can easily create.

Liesbeth Groot Nibbelink and Sigrid Merx, meanwhile, point out that "becoming familiar with the equipment does not simply turn somebody into a good director [or] performing artist."[75] In 2017, for example, 300 hours of video is uploaded to YouTube every minute.[76] Nibbelink and Merx posit that "this draws attention to the need to edit and shape [this] material . . . [and] recursively demands reflection on what kind of education and training are appropriate for the intermedial performer."[77] Sweding is a type of performance that "embraces creative practice involving a number of related and interactive technologies," as it pulls from existing movies for inspiration.[78] Sweding can also be a sort of self-education in aesthetics and technology. Creators need to watch a movie, and keep an eye out for things like use of space, set, camera angles, shot lengths, costumes, and lighting, to swede the movie. These cinematic elements often take a subconscious back seat to entertainment, narrative, action, and dialogue. Sweding thus offers a form of cinematic education that is hands-on, and also allows creators to learn movie-making at their own pace and on their own terms. In this way, sweding is a form of techno-play. Because the focus is on process as much if not more than product, video-makers can learn how to use necessary technologies while make their movie. This learning process is a part of the sweding process; sweders don't *necessarily* need to learn how to use video-making and editing technology before embarking on their project.

At the end of *Be Kind Rewind* sweding brings a neighborhood of people together, in an economically impoverished urban area, and inspires them to make a new movie of their own about the history of their neighborhood. In a similar spirit, Swede Fest is a free yearly festival that was launched in 2008 in Fresno, California, by Roque Rodriguez and Bryan Harley. According to their website, "Swede Fest (now in three locations) is the only film festival dedicated to sweded movies, and it's a great way to promote filmmaking in your community."[79] The promoters encourage readers to "grab your friends and family, browse your DVD or Netflix library, [and] start collecting cardboard boxes from your nearest dumpster, because before you know it Swede Fest 12 will be upon us!"[80] The only rules the festival lists are that all videos should be under four minutes, and the videos should be friendly for all ages. "You can swede *Pulp Fiction*," they state, "just find creative ways to get around the violence, language, and nekkidness." They also suggest that submitters should "embrace the amateur nature of sweding . . . [and] opt to use objects around the house rather than spending any real money. The real genius comes from how your personality and sense of humor shine through. Make these films your own and have fun."[81]

RE: *DIRTY HARRY*—SWEDED

Hi Michael!
Sorry it took me so long to find this sweded movie for you, but I finally did!
http://www.youtube.com/watch?v=Rlzvryf8cBc&feature=youtu.be[82]
- Lynz

Hey Lynz,
As I said, some people have too much time on their hands. But I have to tell ya, I did eat that up with a big spoon the second time I watched it. I wasn't able to breathe, much less eat, from laughing so hard during the first viewing. . . . That was sick, real sick.
Thank you!
~M[83]

NOTES

1. *Be Kind Rewind,* dir. Michel Gondry, perf. Jack Black, Mos Def, New Line Cinema, 2008.
2. Alan Kaprow, "Just Doing," *The Drama Review* 41.3 (1997): 101.
3. Paul Connerton, *How Societies Remember* (New York: Cambridge University Press, 1989), 73–74.
4. Connerton, *How Societies Remember,* 74.
5. Connerton, *How Societies Remember,* 73.
6. Robin Bernstein, *Racial Innocence: Performing American Childhood from Slavery to Civil Rights* (New York: New York University Press, 2011), 13.
7. Bernstein, *Racial Innocence,* loc. 13.
8. Nicolas Bourriaud, *Postproduction* (New York: Lukas & Sternberg, 2002): 19.
9. Bourriaud, *Postproduction,* 53.
10. Irene McGinn, "Making a Blockbuster: Is Hollywood Still Truly a 'Film' Industry?" *Meta Pancakes,* May 13, 2010, accessed Aug. 31, 2013. (Blog has been removed from the internet.)
11. Robert G. Weiner and Shelley E. Barba, *In the Peanut Gallery with Mystery Science Theater 3000: Essays on Film, Fandom, Technology and the Culture of Riffing* (Jefferson, NC: McFarland, 2011), Kindle version, loc. 1689.
12. Weiner and Barba, *In the Peanut Gallery,* loc. 1689.
13. Weiner and Barba, *In the Peanut Gallery,* loc. 1689.
14. Weiner and Barba, *In the Peanut Gallery,* loc. 1700.
15. Weiner and Barba, *In the Peanut Gallery,* loc. 1700.
16. Weiner and Barba, *In the Peanut Gallery,* loc. 1720–27.
17. Weiner and Barba, *In the Peanut Gallery,* loc. 1727.
18. Weiner and Barba, *In the Peanut Gallery,* loc. 1733.
19. Weiner and Barba, *In the Peanut Gallery,* loc. 1746.

20. James Hoberman and Jonathan Rosenbaum, *Midnight Movies* (New York: Basic Books, 1983), 517.
21. Hoberman and Rosenbaum, *Midnight Movies*, 520.
22. Weiner and Barba, *In the Peanut Gallery*, loc. 1759.
23. Hoberman and Rosenbaum, *Midnight Movies*, 272.
24. Weiner and Barba, *In the Peanut Gallery*, loc. 1767.
25. Weiner and Barba, *In the Peanut Gallery*, loc. 1767.
26. Hoberman and Rosenbaum, *Midnight Movies*, 301.
27. Weiner and Barba, *In the Peanut Gallery*, loc. 1772.
28. Sconce, as quoted in Weiner and Barba, *In the Peanut Gallery*, loc. 1778.
29. Sconce, as quoted in Weiner and Barba, *In the Peanut Gallery*, loc. 1778.
30. Hoberman and Rosenbaum, *Midnight Movies*, 306.
31. Hoberman and Rosenbaum, *Midnight Movies*, 311.
32. Hoberman and Rosenbaum, *Midnight Movies*, 328–30. (Emphasis added.)
33. *Be Kind Rewind*, dir. Michel Gondry, perf. Jack Black, Mos Def, New Line Cinema, 2008.
34. *Be Kind Rewind*.
35. Arcadian, "Sweded Films," *Know Your Meme*, accessed July 18, 2012, http://knowyourmeme.com/memes/sweded-films.
36. Arcadian, "Sweded Films."
37. Arcadian, "Sweded Films."
38. Diedre Boyle, "From Portapak to Camcorder: A Brief History of Guerrilla Television," *Journal of Film and Video* 44.1 (1992): 68.
39. Boyle, "From Portapak," 68.
40. Boyle, "From Portapak," 68.
41. Boyle, "From Portapak," 68.
42. Boyle, "From Portapak," 69.
43. Boyle, "From Portapak," 74.
44. Diedre Boyle, "Subject to Change: Guerrilla Television Revisited," *Art Journal* 45.3 (1985): 229.
45. Boyle, "Subject to Change," 229.
46. Brian Rusted, "Portapak as Performance: VTR St-Jacques and VTR Rosedale," in *Challenge for Change*, eds. Thomas Waugh et al (Quebec: McGill-Queen's University Press, 2010), Kindle version, loc. 4440.
47. Rusted, "Portapak as Performance," loc. 4567.
48. Rusted, "Portapak as Performance," loc. 4609.
49. Rusted, "Portapak as Performance," loc. 4629.
50. Rusted, "Portapak as Performance," loc. 4672.
51. Rusted, "Portapak as Performance," loc. 4672.
52. Brian Simpson, "Neverending Story Sweded Extended," *YouTube*, May 14, 2008, accessed Aug. 15, 2013, https://www.youtube.com/watch?v=VJZ1i0L7QlI.
53. Simpson, "Neverending Story Sweded Extended."
54. Email excerpt courtesy of Michael Bowman.
55. Joshua Elliott, "Willy Wonka & The Chocolate Factory Sweded (original 1971)," *YouTube*, Feb. 21, 2008, accessed Aug. 21, 2013, https://www.youtube.com/watch?v=dOwNwsxaW5k.
56. Email excerpt courtesy of Michael Bowman.
57. Deb Margolin, "A Performer's Notes on Parody," *Theatre Topics* 13.2 (2003): 248.
58. Margolin, "A Performer's Notes," 250.
59. Margolin, "A Performer's Notes," 251.
60. Tom Shone, *Blockbuster: How Hollywood Learned to Stop Worrying and Love the Summer* (New York: Free Press, 2004), 146.
61. Shone, *Blockbuster*, 146.
62. Shone, *Blockbuster*, 146.
63. Candice Hopkins, "Making Things Our Own: The Indigenous Aesthetic in Digital Storytelling Author(s)," *Leonardo* 39.4 (2006): 342.

64. Hopkins, "Making Things Our Own," 342.
65. Trinh T. Minh-ha, *Native Woman Other: Writing Postcoloniality and Feminism* (Indianapolis: Indiana University Press, 1989), 122.
66. HCDMediaGroup, "Henry Jenkins," *YouTube,* Sept. 21, 2009, accessed Sept. 22, 2013, https://www.youtube.com/watch?v=ibJaqXVaOaI.
67. Minh-ha, *Native Woman Other,* 122.
68. Conversation paraphrased, courtesy of Lauren Leist.
69. Raymond Johnson, "Trivia," *IMDb,* accessed Aug. 31, 2013, http://www.imdb.com/title/tt0066999/trivia.
70. Johnson, "Trivia."
71. Johnson, "Trivia."
72. Johnson, "Trivia."
73. As of Sept. 2016.
74. Bianca Stigter, as quoted in Liesbeth Groot Nibbelink and Sigrid Merx, "Presence and Perception: Analysing Intermediality in Performance," *Mapping Intermediality in Performance,* eds. Sarah Bay-Cheng et al. (Amsterdam: Amsterdam University Press, 2010), 233.
75. Nibbelink and Merx, "Presence and Perception," 233.
76. "YouTube Company Statistics," *2016 Statistic Brain Research Institute,* n.d., accessed May 17, 2017, http://www.statisticbrain.com/youtube-statistics/.
77. *Nibbelink* and Merx, "Presence and Perception," 233.
78. Nibbelink and Merx, "Presence and Perception," 233.
79. "About Us," *Swede Fest,* accessed Sept. 6, 2013, http://swedefest.com/about-us/.
80. *Swede Fest,* accessed Sept. 6, 2013, http://swedefest.com.
81. *Swede Fest.*
82. This link leads to the version of *Dirty Harry—Sweded* described in this chapter.
83. Email excerpt courtesy of Michael Bowman.

Conclusion: Another Neverending Story

A variation on sweding, Perry Bard's project, "Man with a Movie Camera: The Global Remake," is "a participatory video shot by people around the world who are invited to record images interpreting the original script of Vertov's *Man with a Movie Camera* and upload them" to her website.[1] The project has been ongoing since 2007. According to Bard's website, "software developed specifically for this project archives, sequences and streams the submissions as a film. Anyone can upload footage. When the work streams, each user's contribution becomes part of a worldwide montage, in Vertov's terms the 'decoding of life as it is.'"[2] The website offers each shot in Vertov's 1929 film, and "thumbnails representing the beginning, middle, and end of each shot."[3] Crowdsourcing on a massive scale, Bard invites everyone to "interpret Vertov and upload . . . footage to this site to become part of the database."[4]

The participatory movie is shown on the website in split screen. On the left is Vertov's version. On the right, a new version of the movie is built each day using the crowdsourced clips. Bard states, "the uploaded shots are rotated each day if there is more than one. So the built movie may never be quite the same."[5] Slugs (i.e., black shots) are included in the crowdsourced version, indicating shots still waiting for an adaptation and upload. For crowd inspiration, Bard explains that "Vertov's footage was shot in the industrial landscape of the 20s," and then asks, "What images translate the world today? E.g., instead of the mining scene, if you're living in Silicon Valley you might film inside Apple headquarters."[6] Bard's project includes over 3,000 uploads to date, from 60 countries. Additionally, "the work was named by Google one of the 106 best uses of the internet and won a Guggenheim award as one of the Top 25 for its YouTube Play Biennial."[7]

Vertov's movie, which offers only the barest narrative plot, shows Soviet citizens playing, working, and using modern (i.e., 1920s) machinery. Together, the citizens create a sort of "day in the life" of a fictional Soviet city. However, the citizens, as characters in the film, take second billing to the title's cameraman and the movie editor, whose actions (directorial choices, shots, edits, etc.) emphasize how film can *go anywhere*, and can be manipulated to create fascinating—and possibly deceitful—illusions. This idea was not yet a fact of life in Vertov's time, as it is for many people today. As Vertov wrote of the film, "This new experimentation work by Kino-Eye is directed towards the creation of an authentically international absolute language of cinema . . . on the basis of its complete separation from the language of theatre and literature."[8] While there may be differences in the "languages" of cinema when compared to other arts, the language of cinema (or video) is still forever entwined with theatre and literature. Each art form comes from a basic human impulse to document, create, and share a vision or interpretation of the world with others. Changing the medium or the scale of the vision does not change the impulse to perform the action.

"Man with a Movie Camera: The Global Remake" and Bard's explanations are vivid examples of what Paul Edwards refers to when he states that "adaptation is not a timeless theory or a set of techniques, but a succession of diverse embodied practices, driven by desire and even desperate neediness [to re-tell stories] in one's own time and place."[9] If I were to apply Hutcheon's theory of adaptation modes to this project, I might describe it as a large and unwieldy combination of the showing and interacting modes, with a complicated collective authorship. This description doesn't really help me understand the project, the process, or the point of it all. Further, because the video clips uploaded by each adapter are of very short duration, the project may not even count as adaptation using Hutcheon's theory. Yet, it seems rather obvious that this project uses processes of adaptation, and that it *is* a new adaptation (in the sense of adaptation as product) of an older film that changes day to day.

Using the glossary of strategies I outlined in chapter 1, Bard's project comes closest to sweding—recreating a popular film using what is at hand. More usefully, however, and as much as the final product may seem like (and is titled as) a remake, each clip uploaded to Bard's project could also be classified individually, depending on how the creator chose to adapt his/her piece. By asking internet users to come up with personal and cultural correlations to adapt collectively Vertov's non-narrative film, Bard inspires thought about how present-day technologies are not so different from past technologies—they're just cheaper, more accessible, more convenient, and allow for mass participation (e.g., crowdsourcing) in ways that older technologies do not. Bard's project also shows us to whom the necessary technologies are available, and beyond this, who is driven to use them to participate in the project. If we were to consider who is contributing, clip-by-clip (an undertaking that is beyond the scope of this book), the worldwide project could also reveal—on a large scale—video-making divides (in terms of how skilled the video adapters seem) and digital divides (in terms of where the videos are being uploaded from, and who is doing the uploading).

Additionally, "Man with a Movie Camera: The Global Remake" draws parallels between relatively random contemporary scenes of everyday life and stories from around the world, and the stories that Vertov collected and shared through his film. The act of re-telling *Man with a Movie Camera* in this collective and consistently evolving way implies Edwards' questions: "Why tell this story?" and "Why now?"[10] The project also implies further questions performance studies and adaptation scholars and artists should be quite familiar with: "Why tell this story again?"; "How might we re-tell this story to keep it relevant?"; and "Who is the audience for this re-telling?" The story, the *now*, the relevance, and the audience for Bard's project change day to day, based on life experiences, personal interpretations, available technologies, and who decides to upload video clips to the project.

Man with a Movie Camera, despite Vertov's supposed intentions to use the film to decode "life as it is," still ultimately used only one man's vision to show the ideals of an industrialized Soviet city. Bard's global remake, meanwhile, indeed comes closer to showing "life as it is," as the movie camera is symbolically handed over to anyone who would like to participate. While co-creators are asked to use Vertov's film as a model, they are also explicitly asked, in Bard's project description, to *interpret* Vertov's shots, rather than replicate them. This has resulted in an ever-changing, polyvocal, trans-cultural montage that lacks the ideological cohesiveness of Vertov's original, and this is largely the point. "Life as it is" is a moving target and highly subjective, and the global adaptation captures this essence. Further, though I have been referring to "Man with a Movie Camera: The Global Remake" as "Bard's project," the montage has thousands of co-authors, all credited on the website that Bard authored. Referring to the piece as Bard's project reinforces old models of authorship that the project attempts to invert, and shows how easy it is to fall back on established models of authorship and significance when analyzing newer forms of adaptation. These adaptations should be met on their own terms, with new—still unfixed or undetermined in certain cases—terminology.

Much like the ever-evolving, collective adaptation, "Man with a Movie Camera: The Global Remake," the nature of the other online adaptations I address in this book is that there likely will not ever be a proper *end* to any of my chosen case studies. The examples I use to discuss different methods of video-to-video adaptation may have a limited shelf life. Antoine Dodson and Sweet Brown, like many public figures made famous via YouTube, have likely already seen the apex and (rapid) decline of their popularity. However, specific case studies aside—and to revisit the glossary I outlined in chapter 1—the processes involved in video reenactments, remakes, and remixes have evolved from a long history of performances of re-creation, re-combination, and re-contextualization. These methods of adaptation will undoubtedly persist in video-to-video adaptation, along with other creative forms. Similarly, covering, as homage and/or creating variations on a theme, is an artistic strategy that will probably continue to stand the test of time. Covering, when understood as a "my version of" tribute, rather than just the re-creation of a song, shows that this artistic strategy might also be considered in terms of how it applies to non-musical media. Songification, meanwhile, is specific to music and autotune technology, and thus may prove to be a comparatively short-lived phenomenon. The "-ification," however, might be applied to other types of adaptation that complicate traditional models of authorship, along with the media and genres that are combined in the adaptive process. In December 2013, for example, Paul Little created a two-minute one-man parody of *Home Alone* (1990). Similar to the popular JibJab eCards, where creators can insert still images of faces into videos of dancing elves and reindeer (among many other dancing holiday figures), Little uses still images from *Home Alone* and inserts videos of his face, performing well-known scenes, in the place of the characters' faces.[11] A video of Little's face is superimposed onto a still image of Kevin McCallister (Macaulay Culkin's character) sitting at the dining table, for example. Little smiles and says the line from that moment in the movie: "I made my family disappear!" In a later scene, Little (as Kevin) is looking at a family photo. The camera cuts to the photo: Little has superimposed his face over that of every family member.[12] Following songification, we might call these type of video adaptations something like "selfification." While the terms are equally silly, they denote processes of adaptation for which we did/do not yet have a vocabulary.

Similarly, in September 2013, Leon Mackie and Lilly Lang, along with their infant Orson, began a photo blog called "Cardboard Box Office," which they have continued into 2017. According to Mackie and Lang:

> The project began after finding that we had accumulated both a lot of cardboard boxes (due to moving to a new country) and a baby (due to giving birth). With our social lives drastically altered we decided to find a way to make some of those housebound weekends a little more fun. The costumes, props, and sets in Cardboard Box Office are created entirely out of everyday household items, toys, cardboard, and three individuals slowly losing their sanity.[13]

On the photo blog, Mackie and Lang have uploaded recreated images of famous scenes from popular movies, using cardboard and other cheap arts and crafts materials. The family dons makeshift costumes to play the movie characters in each image. "The Cradle of Doom," for example, is a recreated image of a scene from *Indiana Jones and the Temple of Doom* (1984). The image shows the family packed into the baby's cradle, which looks like an out of control mine cart rolling forward—in no small part due to the parents' facial expressions, and great use of red lighting.[14] In another photo, titled "Wah Wars," the family remakes an image from *Star Wars Episode V: The Empire Strikes Back* (1980). Orson, who holds a wrapping paper roll qua lightsaber, plays Luke Skywalker, while his parents take on the roles of Han Solo and Princess Leia. A teddy bear Chewbacca follows close behind, as they round a corner. In the photo, the menacing shadow of Darth Vader looms on the wall next to where they stand, and Mackie and Lang look up at Vader (whom the viewer cannot see) in horror.[15] Additional stills that Mackie and Lang have recreated include *The Life Aquatic with Steve Zissou* (titled "The Life Domestic"), *The Dark Knight* ("The Dark Nighty-Night"), and *Apollo 13* ("Houston, We Have a Poopy"), among others. Mackie and Lang have continued to create these images as Orson has grown into a toddler. More recent images they've created also insinuate that they were expecting a new baby (who has since been born): in Hollywood terms, *Coming Soon in 2016*. While Mackie and Lang use techniques similar to sweding to create their photos, their adaptations are still photos rather than videos—another process of adaptation for which we don't yet have a term.

Techno-play adaptations, as they are presented in this book, are specific to video technology. Yet techno-play as a process of adaptation might also be applied to any technology that people are learning how to use while simultaneously creating. Response videos are not necessarily as specific to any given technology as they are to the community spirit that exists within certain YouTube circles and subcultures. Response, in this book, is applied to video adaptations, yet it can also work in a variety of media and creative forms.

Additional video adaptation trends that have evolved recently include "Bad Lip Readings" and "Silent" or "Music-less" music videos, in which new (often humorous) sound is added to a popular video or remix of popular videos. These strategies follow in the footsteps of creative subtitling, yet use slightly different methods and technologies. Creative subtitling and sweding, meanwhile, are methods that are specific to video, yet are both borne from longer histories of video (and non-video) parody as celebration and critique. Further, not unlike the Gregory Brothers "Autotune the News" series, internet celebrity Randy Rainbow creates politically and visually savvy videos and songs using his own voice, musical talent, and campy humor (i.e., no autotune technology). Rainbow intercuts his own footage with footage from television news and other sources, so he appears to be interviewing celebrities and political figures over the phone or in person, meanwhile offering his own (sometimes musical) spin on current social and political events.[16] Rainbow's video parodies fall somewhere between remix, response, cover, and something we don't have precise language for yet in performance, film, media, or adaptation studies. Meanwhile, Rainbow's most popular videos have nearly a million views, and his most recent political videos have view counts ranging from 75,000 to 150,000 each—views which accumulated over just a few weeks in May 2017.[17]

Overall, adaptation as processes of change, and adaptation trends, when viewed as personal, cultural, social, and political performances, will persist as long as we have technologies that allow us to copy, adapt, and tell stories—our own, the stories of others, and hybrid stories that merge one individual or group with another to create new meanings. Internet users will continue to adapt stories, with repetitions and variations, using the popular media of the time. New adaptations will be inspired by present-day cultures, and will also have the capacity to inspire changes in these cultures. The video meme is not static, and is not any original piece, but rather consists of all the copies, variations, *adaptations* of the so-called original, as well as the cultural forces that move and spread these adaptations, inspiring others to create and share. Memes and video cameras, as scriptive things, implicitly instruct us how we can and should adapt. The meme serves as a model, while the camera suggests that we point it toward some subject we find interesting and record it.

Yet, in our adaptations, *we* decide what to record, what to keep, what to accentuate, what to change, and what to erase from previous versions. Each decision carries with it creative potential, and potential ethical quandaries. The strategies we use to adapt (parody, camp, music, etc.) will affect whether our versions catch on with larger publics, and how our versions might then be perpetuated, challenged, or changed by others. Michelle Dobyne's "energetic eyewitness account" of an apartment fire in Tulsa, Oklahoma, in January 2016, for example, can be seen as an extension of the way that YouTube users have adapted both the Antoine Dodson and Sweet Brown news interviews.[18] YouTube users have songified, remade, remixed, reenacted, and responded to Dobyne's interview, replicating, changing, and challenging the news interview as a scriptive thing, and drawing parallels between Dobyne's interview performance and Sweet Brown's, particularly in terms of Dobyne's mention of someone with "no shoes," her emphatic facial expressions, and her vocal expressiveness.[19] Finally, the problems and complexities of current US copyright laws, and the way these laws are enforced, will continue to hamper our ability to adapt and share online, lest we figure out additional creative and generative ways to protest (as the Untergangers have, with their *Downfall* adaptations) what are now archaic and too often poorly interpreted laws.

The case studies I discuss in chapters 2 through 5 open up many questions beyond the ones with which I began. In the spirit of adaptation as a cultural force and social undertaking, I will not end, but rather *stop* with these questions, with the hope of inspiring future research, and adaptations of some or all of this book: How can we, with vested interests in the future of performance studies and adaptation, better celebrate everyday creativity and the impulse to make art and make statements that currently lack larger cultural sanctioning? How might we create a greater sense of event, responsibility, and ethics for such everyday adaptations? How can we foster communitas through collective adaptation? How might we de-regulate creativity, and ensure the future lives of creative works that we would like to see grow? How will we justify the liberties that we take, with our adaptations of others' stories? How will we decide what the *next ones* will be, and who gets to help make them? How will we add our voices, our bodies, our visions, and our performances in meaningful and meaning-making ways, to the ever-growing and entangled forests of on- and offline adaptations? Where will we post our versions?

NOTES

1. Perry Bard, "Man With the Movie Camera: The Global Remake," accessed Sept. 5, 2013, http://dziga.perrybard.net.
2. Bard, "Man With the Movie Camera."
3. Bard, "Man With the Movie Camera."
4. Bard, "Man With the Movie Camera."
5. Bard, "Man With the Movie Camera."
6. Bard, "Man With the Movie Camera."
7. Jeff Edwards, "Man with a Movie Camera: The Global Remake by Perry Bard," *Visual & Critical Studies,* Jan. 28, 2012, accessed Sept. 6, 2013, http://vcs.sva.edu/exhibitions/man-with-a-movie-camera-the-global-remake-by-perry-bard/.
8. Dziga Vertov, *Kino-Eye: The Writings of Dziga Vertov* (Berkeley: University of California Press, 1995).
9. Paul Edwards, "Staging Paradox: The Local Art of Adaptation," in *SAGE Handbook of Performance Studies,* eds. D. Soyini Madison and Judith Hamera (Thousand Oaks: Sage, 2006), 233–34.
10. Edwards, "Staging Paradox," 242.
11. Sarah Barness, "Some Guy Named Paul Performs Every 'Home Alone' Part Himself for His Video Christmas Card," *Huffington Post,* Dec. 23, 2013, accessed Jan. 6, 2014, http://www.huffingtonpost.com/2013/12/23/paul-home-alone-christmas_n_4494143.html.
12. Paul Little, "Paul's Home Alone Christmas Card," *YouTube,* Dec. 19, 2013, accessed January 6, 2014, https://www.youtube.com/watch?v=idnXrzDtusA.
13. Leon Mackie and Lilly Lang, "What Is This Cardboard Box Office?" *Cardboard Box Office,* accessed Jan. 2, 2014, https://cardboardboxoffice.com/about/.
14. Leon Mackie and Lilly Lang, "The Cradle of Doom," *Cardboard Box Office,* Oct. 5, 2013, accessed Jan. 2, 2014, https://cardboardboxoffice.files.wordpress.com/2013/11/templeofdoom1.jpg.
15. Leon Mackie and Lilly Lang, "Wah Wars" *Cardboard Box Office,* Sept. 28, 2013, accessed Jan. 2, 2014, https://cardboardboxoffice.files.wordpress.com/2013/11/starwars1.jpg.
16. "Randy Rainbow," 2016, accessed May 18, 2017, http://www.randyrainbow.com.
17. On YouTube, as of May 17, 2017, Randy Rainbow's recent political parodies include "THE RUSSIAN CONNECTION—Randy Rainbow Song Parody," which earned 78,000 views in 3 days; "UNPOPULAR!—Randy Rainbow Song Parody," which earned 147,000 views over two weeks "JUST MY BILL (O'Reilly)—A Randy Rainbow Song Parody," which earned 80,000 views in three weeks, and "Randy Rainbow Interviews Ivanka Trump," which earned 93,000 views over one month. Randy Rainbow, *YouTube,* n.d., accessed May 17, 2017, https://www.youtube.com/user/Tday4U/videos.
18. ColtonW, "Michelle Dobyne/It's Poppin/No Fire, Not Today," *Know Your Meme,* accessed Oct. 30, 2016, http://knowyourmeme.com/memes/michelle-dobyne-it-s-poppin-no-fire-not-today.

19. Michelle Dobyne's news interview can be viewed at https://www.youtube.com/watch?v=KikI_ttYzC4 (Rob Adair, "Michelle Dobyne—NOT TODAY! It's Poppin! Casa Linda Apartments Interview," *YouTube*, Jan. 10, 2016, accessed Oct. 30, 2016). The Gregory Brothers' songified version of Dobyne's interview can be viewed at https://www.youtube.com/watch?v=XpSOWfFtKJE (schmoyoho, "Not Today [The Building Is on Fire] ft. Michelle Dobyne—Songify This," *YouTube*, Jan. 12, 2016, accessed Oct. 30, 2016). Further, an example of a songified remix that draws parallels between Michelle Dobyne's and Sweet Brown's news interviews can be viewed at https://www.youtube.com/watch?v=gH-AxXNJ0GA (WTFBrahh, "The Building Is On Fire REMIX [Feat. Sweet Brown]—WTFBRAHH," *YouTube*, Jan. 12, 2016, accessed Oct. 30, 2016).

Bibliography

8thSin. "Fan Translation Guide." *8thSin Fansubs Anime Blog*. Last modified Mar. 18, 2012. Accessed Oct. 13, 2013.

Alerion. "Hitler's Reaction to the Nyan Cat (Hitler Parody)." YouTube. Last modified June 1, 2011. Accessed Oct. 14, 2013. https://www.youtube.com/watch?v=tDolSn3Xvzc.

Amp. "Hitler Actor Bruno Ganz Interview About Youtube Downfall Parodies." YouTube. Last modified Feb. 21, 2012. Accessed May 19, 2013. https://www.youtube.com/watch?v=4YLqC3DIgjY.

Arcadian. "Sweded Films." *Know Your Meme*. Accessed July 18, 2012. http://knowyourmeme.com/memes/sweded-films.

avidsonicfan1991. "Hitler and His Friends Explain How to Make a PROPER Hitler Parody." YouTube. Last modified Sept. 25, 2012. Accessed July 25, 2013.

Babuscio, Jack. "Camp and the Gay Sensibility," in *Gays and Film*, ed. Richard Dyer. New York: Zoetrope, 1984, 40–57.

Banks, Rodney Oliver. "SWEET BROWN COLD POP INSPIRATIONAL REMIX by Rodney Oliver Banks." *YouTube*. Last modified May 24, 2012. Accessed Sept. 21, 2012.

Bard, Perry. "Man With the Movie Camera: The Global Remake." Accessed Sept. 5, 2013. http://dziga.perrybard.net.

Barness, Sarah. "Some Guy Named Paul Performs Every 'Home Alone' Part Himself for His Video Christmas Card." *Huffington Post*. Last modified Dec. 23, 2013. Accessed Jan. 6, 2014. http://www.huffingtonpost.com/2013/12/23/paul-home-alone-christmas_n_4494143.html.

BarrettTV. "Antoine Dodson Discusses His New Show Based on Bed Intruder." YouTube. Last modified Aug. 27, 2010. Accessed Mar. 31, 2011. https://www.youtube.com/watch?v=pC0naK49Pb8.

———. "Sweet Brown is on Fire! (Parody)." YouTube. Last modified Apr. 11, 2012. Accessed Jan. 14, 2013. https://www.youtube.com/watch?v=tIqs1LbJWgM.

Be Kind Rewind. Dir. Michel Gondry. Perf. Jack Black, Mos Def. New Line Cinema, 2008.

Bernstein, Robin. *Racial Innocence: Performing American Childhood from Slavery to Civil Rights*. New York: New York University Press, 2011.

Bourriaud, Nicolas. *Postproduction*. New York: Lukas & Sternberg, 2002.

Bowman, Michael S. "'Novelizing' the Stage: Chamber Theatre After Breen and Bakhtin." *Text and Performance Quarterly* 15.1 (1995): 1–23.

Boyle, Deirdre. "From Portapak to Camcorder: A Brief History of Guerrilla Television." *Journal of Film and Video* 44.1 (1992): 67–79.

———. "Subject to Change: Guerrilla Television Revisited." *Art Journal* 45.3 (1985): 228–32.

Braudy, Leo. "Afterword: Rethinking Remakes," in *Play It Again, Sam: Retakes on Remakes*, eds. Andrew Horton and Stuart Y. McDougal. Berkeley: University of California Press, 1998.

Breen, Robert S. *Chamber Theatre*. Evanston, IL: Wm. Caxton, 1986.

Brown, Brent. "5-Year-Old Impersonates Sweet Brown." YouTube. Last modified May 13, 2012. Accessed Nov. 16, 2012. https://www.youtube.com/watch?v=_4AxzpYpcn8.

Burgess, Jean. "'All Your Chocolate Rain Are Belong to Us'? Viral Video, YouTube and the Dynamics of Participatory Culture," in *The Video Vortex Reader*, ed. Geert Lovink et al. Amsterdam: Institute of Network Cultures, 2008.

Cavanaugh, Linda. "Sweet Brown Sits Down with Us in Studio." KFOR-TV. Last modified April 16, 2012. Accessed Jan. 14, 2013. http://kfor.com/2012/04/16/sweet-brown-sits-down-with-us-in-studio/.

Charlieville. "Sweet Brown: The New Antoine Dodson." *Break*. Last modified Apr. 11, 2012. Accessed July 24, 2012.

Clark, Katerina, and Michael Holquist. *Mikhail Bakhtin*. Cambridge: Belknap-Harvard University Press, 1984.

Cohen, Julie E. "The Place of the User in Copyright Law." *Fordham Law Review* 74 (2005): 372–74.

ColtonW. "Michelle Dobyne/It's Poppin/No Fire, Not Today," *Know Your Meme*. Last modified May 2016. Accessed Oct. 30, 2016. http://knowyourmeme.com/memes/michelle-dobyne-it-s-poppin-no-fire-not-today.

———. "Sweet Brown/Ain't Nobody Got Time for That." *Know Your Meme*. Accessed Sept. 5, 2016. http://knowyourmeme.com/memes/sweet-brown-aint-nobody-got-time-for-that.

Connerton, Paul. *How Societies Remember*. New York: Cambridge University Press, 1989.

Crazy Laugh Action. "ANTOINE DODSON—FUNNIEST NEWS INTERVIEW EVER (Original)." YouTube. Last modified April 11, 2012. Accessed Sept. 5, 2016. https://www.youtube.com/watch?v=EzNhaLUT520.

Dawkins, Richard. *The Selfish Gene*. Oxford: Oxford University Press, 1976.

Delahaye, Gabe. "Sweet Brown Is OUR Generation's Antoine Dodson." *Videogum*. Last modified Apr. 11, 2012. Accessed July 24, 2012.

Deznell. "SWEET BROWN QUARTET." YouTube. Last modified Apr. 22, 2012. Accessed Sept. 21, 2012. https://www.youtube.com/watch?v=Mfav0yvcaks.

Djheat. "Donnell Rawlings aka Ashy Larry—Bed Intruder Response Song." YouTube. Last modified Aug. 31, 2010. Accessed Sept. 19, 2013. https://www.youtube.com/watch?v=hXjBIu1GPm8.

Dorman, James M. "Shaping the Popular Image of Post-Reconstruction American Blacks: The 'Coon Song' Phenomenon of the Gilded Age." *American Quarterly* 40 (1988): 455.

Downfall. Dir. Oliver Hirschbiegel, Perf. Bruno Ganz. Constantine Films, 2004.

"Downfall Parodies Forum." Accessed Aug. 31, 2016. http://www.downfallparodies.net/forum/.

DrMathRSA's channel. "Hitler Learns He Cannot Divide by Zero." YouTube. Last modified Aug. 23, 2010. Accessed Oct. 13, 2013. https://www.youtube.com/watch?v=FuTz3NL32AM.

Dubs, Jamie. "Downfall/Hitler Reacts." *Know Your Meme*. Accessed July 18, 2012. http://knowyourmeme.com/memes/downfall-hitler-reacts.

Edwards, Jeff. "Man With a Movie Camera: The Global Remake by Perry Bard." *Visual & Critical Studies*. Last modified Jan. 28, 2012. Accessed Sept. 6, 2013. http://vcs.sva.edu/exhibitions/man-with-a-movie-camera-the-global-remake-by-perry-bard/.

Edwards, Paul. "Adaptation: Two Theories." *Text and Performance Quarterly* 27.4 (2007): 369–77.

———. "Adapting Fiction: Chamber Theatre as Criticism of Narrative Structure." *Communication Journal of the Communication Assn. of the Pacific* 11.2 (1982): 77–85.

———. "Staging Paradox: The Local Art of Adaptation," in *SAGE Handbook of Performance Studies*, eds. D. Soyini Madison and Judith Hamera. Thousand Oaks: Sage, 2006, 227–53.

Elliott, Joshua. "Willy Wonka & The Chocolate Factory Sweded (original 1971)." YouTube. Last modified Feb. 21, 2008. Accessed Aug. 21, 2013. https://www.youtube.com/watch?v=dOwNwsxaW5k.

Fagerjord, Anders. "After Convergence: YouTube and Remix Culture," in *International Handbook of Internet Research*, ed. J. Hunsinger et al. New York: Springer Science + Business Media, 2010.

FightingInternet. "Hitler Reacts to SOPA." YouTube. Last modified Dec. 20, 2011. Accessed July 21, 2013. https://www.youtube.com/watch?v=uvXo4sGB7zM.

Fiske, John. *Reading the Popular*. London: Routledge, 1989.

———. *Television Culture*. Padstow: T J Press, 1987.

GubraeTheSecond. "Hitler Gets Rick Rolled." YouTube. Last modified May 6, 2009. Accessed June 5, 2013. https://www.youtube.com/watch?v=LLd2uAam0hI.

Hagerman, Andrew. "Hitler Can't See Avatar." YouTube. Last modified Feb. 5, 2010. Accessed Oct. 13, 2013. https://www.youtube.com/watch?v=j32qsBHS0b8.

———. *Reading the Popular*. London: Routledge, 1989.

Hartley, John. *Television Truths: Forms of Knowledge in Popular Culture*. London: Blackwell, 2008.

HCDMediaGroup. "Henry Jenkins." YouTube. Last modified Sept. 21, 2009. Accessed Sept. 22, 2013. https://www.youtube.com/watch?v=ibJaqXVaOaI.

Heffernan, Virginia. "The Hitler Meme." *The New York Times Magazine*. Last modified Oct. 24, 2008. Accessed July 26, 2012. http://www.nytimes.com/2008/10/26/magazine/26wwln-medium-t.html?_r=0.

heidibell1979. "Sweet Brown Remake by 6yr Old." YouTube. Last modified Nov. 7, 2012. Accessed Nov. 16, 2012. https://www.youtube.com/watch?v=xCc1KIvnngQ.

"History of Downfall Parodies." *Hitler Parody Wiki*. Accessed Oct. 13, 2013. http://hitlerparody.wikia.com/wiki/History_of_Downfall_parodies.

Hitler Rants Parodies. "Hitler Is Informed He is Bruno Ganz." YouTube. Last modified Feb. 24, 2010. Accessed July 21, 2013. https://www.youtube.com/watch?v=SB7hYC3lWa8.

———. "Hitler Is Informed That There Are Two Hitlers." YouTube. Last modified June 27, 2010. Accessed July 21, 2013. https://www.youtube.com/watch?v=LP12x81uYDU.

———. "Hitler Plans to Make a Downfall Parody." YouTube. Last modified Mar. 29, 2010. Accessed May 19, 2013. https://www.youtube.com/watch?v=ua0bniu-aMA.

Hoberman, James, and Jonathan Rosenbaum. *Midnight Movies*. New York: Basic Books, 1983.

"Home." *Tosh.0*. Comedy Partners, 2016.

Hopkins, Candice. "Making Things Our Own: The Indigenous Aesthetic in Digital Storytelling Author(s)." *Leonardo* 39.4 (2006): 341–44.

hooks, bell. *Reel to Real*. New York: Routledge, 1996.

Hu, Bei. "Jefferies Must Pay Fired Trader $1.86 Million, Court Says." *Bloomberg*. Last modified July 8, 2013. Accessed July 21, 2013.

Hutcheon, Linda. *The Politics of Postmodernism*. New York: Routledge, 1989.

———. *A Theory of Adaptation*. London: Routledge, 2012.

JamJamBigLow. "Woman Wakes Up to Find Intruder in Her Bed (Antoine Dodson Spoof)." YouTube. Last modified July 31, 2010. Accessed March 22, 2011.

Jenkins, Henry. *Convergence Culture: Where Old and New Media Collide*. New York: New York University Press, 2006.

———. "'Slash Me, Mash Me, Spread Me . . . " *Confessions of an Aca/Fan*. April 24, 2007. Accessed August 1, 2012. http://henryjenkins.org/2007/04/slash_me_mash_me_but_please_sp.html.

Johnson, Amber. "Antoine Dodson and the (Mis)Appropriation of the Homo Coon: An Intersectional Approach to the Performative Possibilities of Social Media." *Critical Studies in Media Communication* 30.2 (2013): 1–19.

Johnson, Raymond. "Trivia: *Dirty Harry*." *IMDb*. Accessed Aug. 31, 2013. http://www.imdb.com/title/tt0066999/trivia.

Joleigh, Lauryn. "Cocoa Brown (Sweet Brown Parody)." YouTube. Last modified July 29, 2012. Accessed Aug. 20, 2012. https://www.youtube.com/watch?v=xfrbX0dsELU.

Kaprow, Alan. "Just Doing." *The Drama Review* 41.3 (1997): 101–6.

Kennicott, Philip. "Auto-Tune Turns the Operatic Ideal into a Shoddy Joke." *Washington Post*. Last modified Aug. 29, 2010. Accessed Sept. 19, 2013. http://www.washingtonpost.com/wp-dyn/content/article/2010/08/27/AR2010082702197.html.

Kleinhans, Chuck. "Taking Out the Trash: Camp and the Politics of Parody," in *The Politics and Poetics of Camp*, ed. Moe Myer. London: Routledge, 1994.

Leavitt, Alex. "Memes as Mechanisms: How Digital Subculture Informs the Real World." *Futures of Entertainment*. Last modified Feb. 2, 2010. Accessed July 21 2010. http://www.convergenceculture.org/weblog/2010/02/memes_as_mechanisms_how_digita.php.

Lehrman, Sally et al. *Evaluating Media Coverage of Structural Racism Report*. Frisby & Associates, Inc. 2008.

Lessig, Lawrence. *Free Culture: How Big Media Uses Technology and the Law to Lock Down Culture and Control Creativity*. New York: Penguin Group, 2004.

———. *Remix: Making Art and Commerce Thrive in the Hybrid Economy*. New York: Penguin Group, 2010.

LeVan, Michael. "The Digital Shoals: On Becoming and Sensation in Performance." *Text and Performance Quarterly* 32.3 (2012): 209–19.

Liberty University. "Bed Intruder Christmas Carol song-Liberty University (LU) 2010 Christmas Coffeehouse." YouTube. Last modified Dec. 13, 2010. Accessed Sept. 5, 2016. https://www.youtube.com/watch?v=RMB10wwmWrU.

Linkins, Jason. "The 'Downfall' Internet Meme Has FINALLY Made Somebody Rich." *The Huffington Post*. Last modified July 9, 2013. Accessed July 21, 2013. http://www.huffingtonpost.com/2013/07/09/downfall-internet-meme_n_3568221.html.

Little, Paul. "Paul's Home Alone Christmas Card." YouTube. Last modified Dec. 19, 2013. Accessed January 6, 2014. https://www.youtube.com/watch?v=idnXrzDtusA.

Lott, Eric. *Love and Theft: Blackface Minstrelsy and the American Working Class*. New York: Oxford University Press, 1993.

Lucasmarr. "Sweet Brown: No Time for Bronchitis." YouTube. Last modified Apr. 9, 2012. Accessed July 18, 2012. https://www.youtube.com/watch?v=JaAd8OuwwPk.

Luvvyheart. "Antoine Dodson African Parody." YouTube. Last modified Aug. 12, 2010. Accessed Mar. 22, 2011.

MacDonald, J. Fred. *Blacks and White TV: African Americans in Television Since 1948*. 2nd ed. Chicago: Nelson-Hall, 1992.

Mackie, Leon and Lilly Lang. *Cardboard Box Office*. Accessed Jan. 2, 2014. https://cardboardboxoffice.com/about/.

Margolin, Deb. "A Performer's Notes on Parody." *Theatre Topics* 13.2 (2003): 247–52.

McAlisterMania. "BED INTRUDER Antoine Dodson: Country Version." YouTube. Last modified Aug. 1, 2010. Accessed Mar. 23, 2011.

McGinn, Irene. "Making a Blockbuster: Is Hollywood Still Truly a 'Film' Industry?" *Meta Pancakes*. Last updated May 13, 2010. Accessed Aug. 31, 2013.

MessyMyles. "Sweet Brown's Cold Pop Escape (Spoof)." YouTube. Last modified Apr. 12, 2012. Accessed Aug. 20, 2012. https://www.youtube.com/watch?v=GMRD6kqEB8E.

Michielsen, Kevin. "Sweet Eli Brown." YouTube. Last modified July 30, 2012. Accessed Nov. 16, 2012. https://www.youtube.com/watch?v=uxIaRnVIlJo.

Minh-ha, Trinh T. *Native Woman Other: Writing Postcoloniality and Feminism*. Bloomington: Indiana University Press, 1989.

Morson, Gary Saul and Caryl Emerson. *Mikhail Bakhtin: Creation of a Prosaics*. Stanford: Stanford University Press, 1990.

Natesvlogs. "Employee Evaluation: Sweet Brown Shames Black People." YouTube. Last modified Apr. 13, 2012. Accessed Nov. 20, 2012.

Nelson, B. "Sweet Brown: No Time for Bronchitis (Toddler Parody)." YouTube. Last modified Nov. 5, 2012. Accessed Nov. 16, 2012.

Nibbelink, Liesbeth Groot, and Sigrid Merx. "Presence and Perception: Analysing Intermediality in Performance," in *Mapping Intermediality in Performance*, eds. Sarah Bay-Cheng et al. Amsterdam: Amsterdam University Press, 2010.

NikkieDe. "Nicole Got JOKES: L. Jenkins (News Parody) PART 2." YouTube. Last modified Apr. 13, 2012. Accessed Sept. 19, 2013. https://www.youtube.com/watch?v=_fqyuflV93g.

Nordvall, Andy. "Hitler Is Fed Up with All the Hitler Rants!" YouTube. Last modified Mar. 15, 2009. Accessed July 25, 2012. https://www.youtube.com/watch?v=7vMUvgce_5s.

Offenhuber, Dietmar. *Transformative Copy*. MS Thesis, Media Arts and Sciences, School of Architecture and Planning, Massachusetts Institute of Technology, 2008.

Oshacueru. "ANTOINE DODSON THE RICH WHITE RACIST." YouTube. Last modified Aug. 4, 2010. Accessed Mar. 22, 2011.

Parker, Soalric. "Hitler Rants About Miley Cyrus." YouTube. Last modified Aug. 27, 2013. Accessed Oct. 13, 2013. https://www.youtube.com/watch?v=iYZRsL6ie4A.

The Parody Factory. "Sweet Brown—Ain't Nobody Got Time for That (Autotune Remix)." YouTube. Last modified Apr. 13, 2012. Accessed Sept. 21, 2012. https://www.youtube.com/watch?v=bFEoMO0pc7k.

Plankhead. "Hitler Reacts to the Hitler Parodies Being Removed from YouTube." YouTube. Last modified Apr. 20, 2010. Accessed June 19, 2013. https://www.youtube.com/watch?v=kBO5dh9qrIQ.

poeticstarlet94. "Sweet Brown COGIC Remix." YouTube. Last modified Apr. 25, 2012. Accessed Sept. 21, 2012.

"Randy Rainbow." Last modified May 2017. Accessed May 18, 2017. http://www.randyrainbow.com.

"Relevant Dates in US Copyright." *Express Permissions*. Accessed Sept. 19, 2013. http://www.expresspermissions.com/rel_date.html.

Reublin, Richard A., and Robert L. Maine. "Question of the Month: What Were Coon Songs?" *Jim Crow Museum of Racist Memorabilia Website*. Ferris State University. Last modified May 2005. Accessed Oct. 1, 2013. http://www.ferris.edu/HTMLS/news/jimcrow/question/may05/index.htm.

ReviewManify. "Sweet Brown: No Time for Bronchitis Cold Pop Escape (Parody)." YouTube. Last modified Apr. 12, 2012. Accessed Aug. 20, 2012.

Rogers, Paul. "Streisand's Home Becomes Hit on Web." *San Jose Mercury News*. Last modified June 24, 2003. Accessed July 29, 2012.

Román, David. *Acts of Intervention: Performance, Gay Culture, and AIDS*. Bloomington: Indiana University Press, 1998.

Rosenblum, Emma. "The Director of *Downfall* Speaks Out on All Those Angry YouTube Hitlers." *Vulture*. Last modified Jan. 15, 2010. Accessed July 21, 2013. http://www.vulture.com/2010/01/the_director_of_downfall_on_al.html.

Rusted, Brian. "Portapak as Performance: VTR St-Jacques and VTR Rosedale," in *Challenge for Change*, eds. Thomas Waugh et al. Quebec: McGill-Queen's University Press, 2010.

Salvato, Nick. "Out of Hand: YouTube Amateurs and Professionals." *The Drama Review* 53.3 (2009): 67–83.

Schechner, Richard. *Between Theatre and Anthropology*. Philadelphia: University of Pennsylvania Press, 1985.

Schneider, Rebecca. *Performing Remains: Art and War in Times of Theatrical Reenactment*. New York: Routledge, 2011.

Scott, Kevin. "Sparkle Johnson: No Time For Gay/Sweet Brown no time for bronchitis." YouTube. Last modified Apr. 20, 2012. Accessed Aug. 20, 2012. https://www.youtube.com/watch?v=5fnuKPBrpSk.

Shone, Tom. *Blockbuster: How Hollywood Learned to Stop Worrying and Love the Summer*. New York: Free Press, 2004.

ShortFunnyAsian. "Antoine Dodson—Woman Wakes Up to Find Intruder in Her Bed (PARODY)." YouTube. Last modified Aug. 4, 2010. Accessed June 22, 2012.

Simpson, Brian. "Neverending Story Sweded Extended." YouTube. Last modified May 14, 2008. Accessed Aug. 15, 2013. https://www.youtube.com/watch?v=VJZ1i0L7QlI.

Sirucek, Stefan. "ATTI: Auto Tune the Interview." *The Huffington Post*. Last modified July 6 2010. Accessed March 23, 2011. http://www.huffingtonpost.com/stefan-sirucek/atti-auto-tune-the-interv_b_649113.html.

SmartBoiiable. "No Time for Bronchitis (spoof)." YouTube. Last modified June 26, 2012. Accessed Aug. 21, 2012. https://www.youtube.com/watch?v=lBAVLurDVeY.

SophiaPetrillosBuddy. "Mary J. Blige Burger King Commercial." YouTube. Last modified April 4, 2012. Accessed Jan. 14, 2013. https://www.youtube.com/watch?v=XukHU8y5GRQ.

Spencer, Greg. "Pepsi Next Commercial: Sweet Brown Parody." YouTube. Last modified May 10, 2012. Accessed Aug. 20, 2012. https://www.youtube.com/watch?v=OXgGs6qqOQg.

StatusMusicDesign. "Ain't Nobody Got Time for That (Less Than 1 min. Acoustic . . . Parody?)." YouTube. Last modified June 25, 2012. Accessed Sept. 20, 2013. https://www.youtube.com/watch?v=wMVCOPgKPz4.

Steuver, Hank. "Comedy Central's 'Tosh.0': Five Years Later, It Hurts So Good." *The Washington Post*. Last modified Feb. 15 2014. Accessed May 3, 2015.

Swede Fest. "About Us." Accessed Sept. 6, 2013. http://swedefest.com/about-us/.

Taylor, Yuval, and Jake Austen. *Darkest America: Black Minstrelsy from Slavery to Hip-Hop*. New York: Norton, 2012.

Temple, Krystal. "What Happens in an Internet Minute?" *InsideScoop*. Last modified March 13, 2012. Accessed Sept. 5, 2013. https://scoop.intel.com/what-happens-in-an-internet-minute/.

Toledo, Valerie. "Sweet Brown Remix (Ain't Nobody Got Time for That) Music Video by the Arnaiz Crew." YouTube. Last modified Aug. 26, 2012. Accessed Sept. 21, 2012. https://www.youtube.com/watch?v=vFUrbgGLa6s.

Tosh, Daniel. "Web Redemption–Sweet Brown." *Tosh.0*. Accessed Jan. 14, 2013. http://tosh.comedycentral.com/video-clips/web-redemption---sweet-brown.

Turner, Victor. *The Anthropology of Performance*. New York: PAJ Publications, 1988.

Vertov, Dziga. *Kino-Eye: The Writings of Dziga Vertov*. Berkeley: University of California Press, 1995.

Ward, Elijah G. "Homophobia, Hypermasculinity and the US Black Church." *Culture, Health & Sexuality* 7.5 (2005): 493–504.

Warren, Christina. "How YouTube Fights Copyright Infringement." *Mashable*. Last modified Feb. 17, 2012. Accessed Oct. 13, 2013. http://mashable.com/2012/02/17/youtube-content-id-faq/#0pPsfN6AD5qa.

Weber, Rachel. "Cat Meme Creators in Legal Battle with *Scribblenauts*." *GamesIndustry International*. Last modified May 3, 2013. Accessed Oct. 13, 2013. http://www.gamesindustry.biz/articles/2013-05-03-cat-meme-creators-in-legal-battle-with-scribblenauts.

Weiner, Robert G., and Shelley E. Barba. *In the Peanut Gallery with Mystery Science Theater 3000: Essays on Film, Fandom, Technology and the Culture of Riffing*. Jefferson, NC: McFarland, 2011.

Wilson Marshall, Juli, and Nicholas J. Siciliano. "The Satire/Parody Distinction in Copyright and Trademark Law—Can Satire Ever Be a Fair Use?" ABA Section of Litigation, Intellectual Property Litigation Committee Roundtable Discussion Online. Accessed July 16, 2012. https://apps.americanbar.org/litigation/committees/intellectual/roundtables/0506_outline.pdf.

Winfrey Harris, Tammi. "Move Over, Antoine Dodson! The Ironically Racist Internet Presents Sweet Brown." *Clutch Magazine*. Last modified Apr. 10, 2012. Accessed July 24, 2012.

———. "What's so Funny About Antoine Dodson?" *Change.org News*. Last modified Aug. 24, 2010. Accessed Aug. 1, 2012.

Worthrom, Jenna. "From Viral Video to Billboard 100." *The New York Times*. Last modified Sept. 5, 2010.

Yarbrough, Paige. "Sweet Brown Remake." YouTube. Last modified July 31, 2012. Accessed Nov. 11, 2012. https://www.youtube.com/watch?v=WJnx2_kgb-Q.

Youstillamazeme. "Sweet Brown ('Ain't Nobody Got Time for That' Remix)." YouTube. Last modified Apr. 12, 2012. Accessed Sept. 21, 2012.

"YouTube Company Statistics." *2016 Statistic Brain Research Institute*. n.d. Accessed May 17, 2017.

Index

About the Author

Lyndsay Michalik Gratch is a scholar-artist and an assistant professor of film at Georgia Gwinnett College in Lawrenceville. She earned her PhD in communication studies (with a focus in performance studies) from Louisiana State University in Baton Rouge. Her research and creative interests include performance studies, cinema studies, theatrical and digital adaptation, new media studies, critical/cultural studies, remix culture, visual culture, performative writing, and video art. She has published essays, videos, scripts, and creative writing in *Text & Performance Quarterly*, *Liminalities: A Journal of Performance Studies*, *Theatre Annual*, *The Brooklyn Review*, and *Electric Literature's* "The Outlet."